Questions?

email Pcloudman@aol.com

The God Experience

Opening Your Mind to The Greatest Living Force in The Universe

Perry Smith

authorHOUSE®

AuthorHouse™ LLC
1663 Liberty Drive
Bloomington, IN 47403
www.authorhouse.com
Phone: 1-800-839-8640

Published by AuthorHouse 02/13/2014

ISBN: 978-1-4259-5759-9 (sc)
ISBN: 978-1-4670-8989-0 (e)

This book is printed on acid-free paper.

I Dedicate this book to all people, everywhere . . .
no exceptions

ACKNOWLEDGEMENTS

To my Father who demonstrated to me that a man can be gentle, loving and kind and still be a strong man; my Mother who despite our many differences, gave me love unconditionally; my soul mate Katherine for being my friend, lover and perfect partner; my daughters Susannah and Olivia who taught me how to give love unconditionally; my best friend Steve who has always provided me with true friendship and showed me the way to God; my sister Leslie, it's nice being sister and brother *and* friends; my brother Forrest, I wish we could have spent more time together; my best friends and soul brothers Matthew Antczak (Set the Controls for the Heart of the Sun), Scott Senter (Pass the gravy), Ron Sturgis (How 'Bout them Cowboys) and Nathan Zane (Play that flute!). Members of The Carifio, Smith and Averill families past and present; John Rheaume, Dave Mitchell, Brian Palmerino and all the other "cats" who have passed through The Band; the Jazz Committee; Senter Auto Supply ownership, employees and customers. As great as it is to know God, I have found that it is just as important to have good people in our lives and I have been fortunate to have an abundance of them. And to all my friends and family and acquaintances for all that you have given me I say this from the bottom of my soul, Thank You! I hope I have given something back to you.

Contents

PROLOGUE

The human being is an amazing creature. Just look around you. The wonders of architecture, engineering and construction surround us. Science, technology and medicine have given us knowledge, health and a better quality of living. Humor brings us laughter and relief. Art, music, film and literature has brought joy and beauty to our lives; it has entertained as well as *informed* us. Religion and philosophy has inspired and enlightened us. Philanthropy and charity has helped millions of people in need. There is simply no denying that when we are at our best, there is nothing that we cannot achieve. But it's when we are *not* at our best that brings me to the pages of this book.

It is of vital importance that there are people in this world who speak out, stand up, protest, blow whistles, raise red flags and call attention to the myriad of problems both actual and potential, that exist in this world today. And to all the people who possess the strength and courage to do so I say to you, Bravo! And to all the men and women throughout history as well as today, right now on the front lines who are risking life and limb and in some cases making the ultimate sacrifice to rid this world of hate and violence, intolerance and bigotry, terror and abuse, tyranny and oppression, injustice and inequality, you have given so very much to all of us who value freedom and embrace "life, liberty and the pursuit of happiness." You've made this world a better place for all of humanity and I say to you a million times, *Thank You.* I am now and forever more grateful for your service and sacrifice.

The purpose of this book is not to criticize others or to call attention to the many, many *problems* that exist in this world. Its purpose is to be part of the *solution*: to educate, enlighten and inspire. Yes indeed people *are* amazing but we are *better* when we work *together.* We are better when we have love, wisdom and support *around* us and as you will soon read, *within us.*

It is true that hardships make us stronger and wiser. It is not suppose to be a life of ease for we would be prone to become lazy and stagnant but there is so much, *too much* unnecessary pain and suffering caused but a lack of love for one another as well as unwise, unspiritual and selfish personal choices. With that said, I've known for a very long time now, Someone who possesses an inexhaustible amount of love and wisdom and is eager to share them both with you. I know Someone who wants to be involved intimately in your life and serve you. I know Someone who is not just good but *perfect* in every way, shape and form. And Someone who *every human being* who walks the face of this earth has access to. And through this book, I would like to introduce you *personally* to this most amazing and incredible *Someone*.

The world today is broken and divided and in serious need of love, wisdom, peace, and unity. The world today is ripe for real growth and *deep significant change* and I can't think of anything other than *true spirituality* that is capable of fueling the kind of growth and change that is so desperately needed in this world *right now*. There *will be* a spiritual awakening in this world: a spiritual re-birth. Only this time it will be *rooted* in the rich soil that is the *living experience* of knowing and working with God on a personal, intimate level. And wouldn't it be nice to not only witness this new age but to also be a part of it?

NOTE TO THE READER

In February of 2012, I made a decision to revise and essentially re-write the book you are now reading. It was originally published in the fall of 2006. This new book is the result of that endeavor.

Also, I wish to apologize to anyone who may be a connoisseur of writing and literature. This book is not poetry or a great literary work of art. It has holes and mistakes and is flawed in many ways like I am but above all it is *real*, *honest* and *true*: every single word of it and furthermore, I believe it accurately conveys, in an accessible, down-to-earth fashion, what it *means* to have a living relationship with God and what it *takes* to actually find Him. And while I suppose it could be used for group study, I feel it is best served as a one-on one (writer to reader) experience for the emphasis here is placed on *personal experience/relationship*. This book may not be for everyone but *God is for everyone*. In the end however, from my perspective, this book is only as good as its ability to help the reader find and experience God Himself.

Whatever your measure of good book is, still it is ink and glue, wood pulp and sometimes leather. You cannot live inside of a book in the same way that cannot live inside of a classroom. Books are not alive. They cannot love you. They do not cherish you. They cannot hold and embrace you. People certainly can love and embrace you and God is *incapable* of anything less. The purpose of this book is the same as it was the first time around. First to *expose*, you the reader, to spiritual truth and secondly, if you are willing to take that *giant leap*, discover and experience God for *yourself*. If you are sound and established spiritually, Great! Fantastic! You don't need this book in the same way someone who is happily married has no need for a dating service. But, if you are *not* satisfied spiritually; if you are someone who is *single* and *seeking*; if you are religiously frustrated or even mildly curious about the meaning of true spirituality; if your looking for a deeper well and higher road; if you think that knowing God should be more than a conceptual belief, *you* are the person I wrote this book for.

And my hope is that it will be the avenue that not only takes you to the front porch but that it also helps you to open *your* front door to the Greatest Living Force in the Universe.

When I look at my life I see it in two parts, my life before I found God, and my life after I found God . . .

BEFORE GOD

Beginnings

It all began when Forrest met Delores . . .

Forrest Van Zant Smith II, the youngest of three children, was born November 9, 1922 in Haverhill Massachusetts. His parents, both of English decent, were Forrest Van Zant Smith Sr. and Blanche Robbins. His father was a prominent figure in Haverhill even becoming mayor of the city in the late 1920's. They were a wealthy family until they lost most of their money during the stock market crash of 1929. And although it changed their lives in a material sense, it didn't change them in a deeply profound way because what the Smith family did not lose on that Black Sunday was their *love* for each another.

Growing up, young Forrest developed a love for music and aviation. Practicing along with 78rpm records, he acquired enough musical ability to participate in jam sessions with fellow musicians. This love of playing and music was something he would enjoy throughout his lifetime. It was around this same time that he became an avid modeler. With a keen eye and a steady hand, he produced a rather impressive collection of model airplanes. This is perhaps what inspired him to take to the skies and begin flying lessons. In 1940 he graduated high school and enlisted in the military with hopes of becoming a Naval Aviator. He completed his flight training in July of 1943 and went on to become a Navy fighter pilot based in the Pacific Theater of Combat.

*Lt. (j.g.) Forrest V. Z. Smith, Jr.,age 22, son of former mayor and Mrs. Forrest V. Z. Smith, 13 Fernwood ave., Bradford, has been awarded a Navy air medal and given a citation for meritorious achievement in the Battle of the Marianas last June 19.

Lieutenant Smith is now recovering at the Chelsea Naval hospital from a fractured skull and other injuries received in an automobile accident in this city a few weeks ago while home on leave.

This citation, presented to him at the hospital, credited him with aiding in the destruction of a Jap dive-bomber which had closed in on a naval task force. Lieutenant Smith was pilot on a carrier-based fighter plane and previous to the destruction of the dive bomber has destroyed a Jap reconnaissance plane.

"He materially contributed to the complete failure of the enemy attack," according to the citation, "and his skill and courage were at all times in keeping with the highest traditions of the U. S. Naval service."

*Newspaper Article

When the war was over, in which he served admirably, Forrest married his high school sweetheart Shirley. She gave birth to a son, Forrest Van Zant Smith III on February 9, 1946. It was only a few months later that tragedy struck when the car he was driving, with his wife and child inside, got into a terrible accident. Fortunately, the baby was unharmed. Forrest sustained severe injuries that took him many months to recover from. His young wife however, was killed. This tragic event caused him a great deal of physical and emotional pain. The accident was something he was always reluctant to talk about and for very good reason.

Picking up the pieces of his now broken life, He left his young son in the care of his deceased wife's parents and went back into aviation. After serving his country once again (The Korean War) he began to work as a commercial pilot. This consisted of shuttling small groups, mostly business people, over short distances in small aircraft. It was while performing this job that tragedy struck Forrest once again. While attempting to land his plane during an intense fog on what he thought was a runway, he landed smack-dab into the icy cold waters of Boston Harbor. He and another passenger managed to exit the damaged aircraft that sank in a matter of seconds. Unfortunately, the other passenger/s had no time or were simply too incapacitated to escape and perished. Forrest now found himself in cold water with poor visibility and with a person who could not swim. His passenger told him, "Let me go and save yourself," but Forrest would have none of that. His response was, "Either we get through this together or we die together." It wasn't until the fog cleared when a woman who was outside hanging laundry noticed the two men in the water. She called her husband who quickly grabbed his rowboat and rescued the two men from drowning. It would take quite sometime for Forrest to get over this event but he would one day take to the skies again and resume his passion for flying. This time it would be purely for recreation.

With the past behind him, Forrest now looked to settle down and begin life anew. After working briefly as a car salesman, he began a job as a patent maker for a shoe company. It was also around this time that he met the woman who would become his second wife and my mother.

Delores Ann Carifio was born to Italian immigrants Geogiento (Sharkey) Carifio and Filamena Uzzi in Haverhill, Massachusetts on April 5, 1930. Geogiento owned and operated a local "roadhouse" and also worked as a part-time prizefighter. Filamena was a full-time mother and homemaker. Delores was the youngest in a family of seven boys and two girls. Times were hard for many families during the Great Depression, but like the Smith family, what the Carifio's lack in treasure they made up for with love and family unity. She graduated high school in June of 1948 and immediately went to work for a local electric company. But her true ambition, like many of her generation, was to become a wife, mother and homemaker. She met my father at an officer's party in 1959, but nothing became of it for at that time for she had another man in her life. When her relationship with this man failed to blossom into marriage, she once again met my father and this time, the two went on a date. After a one-year courtship, Forrest and Delores were married in October of 1962. After living in a small apartment, they purchased a modest two-bedroom ranch in a small town just north of the Massachusetts border. This is where they would start their family.

On April 5, 1964, Delores gave birth to a healthy seven pound baby girl they named Leslie Robbins Smith. Almost fifteen months to the day later the couple had their second child, a son. Perry Cloudman Smith, named after Forrest's best friend in the Navy, was born on June 30, 1965. This is where my story begins . . .

It's a Boy

My earliest memory was also a milestone in the life of any young child: waking up with a dry diaper. I remember feeling so very proud. It was not long after this that my mother enrolled me at a local preschool. It was during my time at school that I became aware of the fact that I was a very shy and timid individual *socially*. In class, I was content to be quiet, observe, listen and take directions. My memories from this period in my life are few except for one very significant event that took place at this school: my first moral decision.

The entire kindergarten class had drawn pictures and the teacher had hung them all on the wall to display them. We had not put our names on them so when it came time to take the drawings and bring them home, the teacher had to ask each student which picture belonged to them. Now as she is moving down the line, I see this really cool drawing that I really wanted but it wasn't the picture that I had drawn. As my mind is reeling with decision, the teacher finally gets down to me and asks, "Perry, which one of these pictures is yours?" To be honest, I don't recall which picture I chose but what made this event so memorable was that it was my first real choice between right and wrong. The occasion stills resonates within me some forty years later. Do you recall your first moral decision?

I began my elementary school tenure in the fall of 1971. First grade was held in an old church just about a stones throw away from our house. Grades two thru five were taught at a larger school, which just happens to be "the oldest standing co-ed school in the nation", that was still only a short distance from home. My sister and I would often walk or rides our bikes there. Times were good and I was steadily growing. At school, I was average academically but I was making new friends and learning basic social behavior. But it was in first grade where I made a most monumental discovery: the opposite sex. This one girl in particular had blonde hair, blues eyes and was very pretty. I was aggressive in my pursuit of her even going so far as trying to call her on the telephone. My determination was very surprising considering that only a few short years later, I would become a tongue-tied blubbering mess around girls.

Around the age of six or seven I began attending Sunday School for the purpose of making first communion, which I did. The only memory I have from that experience was drawing pictures. Growing up, religion had little, if any, impact on my life and our household. My mother would call herself a Catholic and my father called himself a Protestant, but you would never know it. Neither of them attended church regularly or practiced any kind of religious ceremony or ritual other than Christmas and Easter and even during these celebrations there were never any overt spiritual messages. But with that being said, my parents were good, kind, caring and loving people who were *completely devoted* to my sister and me and that was all that really mattered.

My image of God at that time basically came from Hollywood movies and Old Testament biblical stories. Films and tales about The Great Flood, The Ten Commandments, the parting of the Red Sea, people turning into salt and burning bushes were all that I knew about religion. God in my mind was an old Caucasian male with a long white beard and long flowing white robe. He would sit on a golden throne with a lightning bolt in one hand and a book of law in the other. God was basically good but you wouldn't want to get Him* angry or else you would be in big trouble. God was someone to be feared rather than someone to be embraced. He was a wise man with a bad temper. But as vague and unclear as my concepts of God were at that time, the funny thing was I never doubted God's *existence*. But I would on occasion test that existence. I would do this by rolling a coin down the middle of the floor. If the coin veered right, He was there in the room with me. Or I would ask God to fill my empty coin-collecting book with rare coins. Even though I would give Him a few minutes, the case would always be empty. But all those things never dampened my "belief" that God was real and essentially good and I found it comforting to know that there someone who was truly "watching over me".

* In the first edition of this book, I when out of my way not to assign gender to God mainly because it does not apply. God transcends gender in the same way peace, love, wisdom, and unity do. Over the centuries, God has been given many titles but for the sake of historical continuity plus the fact that I personally think of God as "The Father", I will refer to God as He/Him in this book as opposed to It or something else. What we choose to address God or think of God as can be personal but who, what and where God is, is universal, timeless and *absolute*.

Home life around this time was, from my vantage point, a cocoon of safety, consistency and love. My mother was the consummate caretaker who was always there for us whether it was the middle of the day or the middle of the night. My father was my absolute hero. He was a real living breathing WWII fighter pilot and I would listen to him for hours talk about his exploits in the Navy during the Great War. And it didn't take long for me to develop a real passion for all things relating to war and the military. Especially modeling. Almost all of my playtime revolved around me being an army soldier or fighter pilot. I would spend hours creating battle scenes with my model airplanes and toy soldiers. My love of all things military prompted me to join a youth organization called the Cub Scouts. The things that appealed to me most about the organization were the uniform and patches. After the thrill of the image wore off and it was time to get down to actual scout business, I quickly became disinterested and quit. This would become a trend with me when it came to organized activities and formal instruction.

Upon entering the third grade during the fall of 1973, my world as well as my understanding of "The" world began to expand. I recall being absolutely shocked to hear from kids at school that families moved around and that parents sometimes split and separated. I couldn't fathom either of those things happening to my family, but it wouldn't be long before one of them (divorce) would become a very real and distinct possibility.

Around this time I noticed that there was something seriously wrong at home that I was totally unaware of when I was younger: my father had a serious drinking problem. And by now it was beginning to rear its ugly head. My sister and I would be playing outside only to see Dad's 1972 Pinto swerving all over the road as he was coming home from work. Other times he would pull into the driveway and miss it altogether running into rocks and over shrubs. It's a small wonder he never hit anyone or got into a serious car accident. Then there were the times inside our house and the vicious arguments between he and my mother. These incidents were the most painful for me because I feared he would become violent and actually hit her. My dad was my hero, but I remember clearly thinking to myself, "Don't you dare lay a finger on my Mother." To my knowledge, he never did. My father never believed that physical violence was an effective way to solve problems.

These hard times didn't last very long because my mother soon issued him this ultimatum: stop the drinking or lose your family. It was right then and there that my father quit drinking, stone cold turkey. I never saw him drunk or take another drink of alcohol again. Looking back on his history and all that he had been through in life, this must have been a monumental struggle (as it is for many of those who endure the hardships of war or have lost a loved-one) as well as an epic triumph for him. I am extremely proud of my father for what he accomplished in turning his own life and with that the life of *our family*, completely around.

Life is Good Again

With my father back on the right track, life at home felt good and safe again. A typical Saturday would start with me going out to breakfast with my dad and then to a nearby hobby shop to purchase mostly 1/72 scale WWI model fighter planes. Later in the day we would assemble them to the music of Charlie Parker and smell of black coffee and Camel cigarettes. When the weather was good, my mom would take me fishing to one of the many area lakes and ponds. Time after school was spent playing with the neighborhood kids. The woods behind our houses were like shopping malls of nature with all kinds of natural treasures and the little ponds and streams were our arcades. We'd catch frogs and tadpoles and fish for kibbies and perch. We'd scour the ground for insects, worms, snakes and salamanders then place them all in a small container to see what would happen. Another activity of ours would be to dig a small hole in the ground, gather up some small braches and start little campfires. There was something very soothing about sitting in front of and tending to a fire. We could get lost for hours just feeling the warmth of the fire and staring into the flames. Fortunately, we were cautious enough not to burn the woods down. Most days during the summer months were spent at the ocean. Mom would pack the car in the morning with food, towels, chairs and maybe an umbrella and my sister and I would each get to take a friend to go spend a long, fun filled day at the beach. We would spend hours riding waves, building sand castles and collecting seashells. And on our way home, we'd stop for a lobster roll and ice cream. It was a great way to spend a summer's day.

At elementary school, I was making new friends, getting good grades and discovering a natural ability I possessed: painting and drawing. I was "the man" when it came to art and I enjoyed my lofty status. It was also here at elementary school where I got into my first and only fight. I had always shied away from the slightest hint of violence and my combatant could probably sense this (it is this fear of confrontation that would lead to my being bullied a few years later). It all happened so quickly and what this fight was over, I still have no clue. I remember being shocked and stunned when *she* (I am not kidding) suddenly lunged at me. The next thing I knew we were both rolling around on the ground and then minute later we were both in tears in the principle's office. To me it was a senseless affair and one I hoped I would never have to experience again.

It was also during this period in my life that I began a lifelong love affair with music. I had always enjoyed listening to the A.M. radio hits of the day, but it was a new T.V. sitcom that would open my ears to a whole new different world of music.

During the mid 1970's, the hit T.V. series "Happy Days" (Based on the life of a middle class American family during the 1950's) had a huge influence on me in two ways. One, it gave me a glimpse into adolescent life and second, it introduced me to the rock and roll music of the 1950's. I remember being immediately drawn to the basic chord structure as well as the raw primal energy of its rhythm and blues influences. Many punk bands during the 70's and beyond were moved by these same musical attributes. Suddenly, I found myself buying and collecting 45rmp records by the likes of Chuck Berry, Bobby Darin, Little Richard,

Jerry Lee Lewis and of course the King of Rock and Roll himself, Elvis Aaron Presley. What fun it was using a tennis racket for a guitar and floor lamp as a microphone to pretend I was the King in performing in front of the entire school. It would be a couple more years before another T.V. show would change my taste in music as well as my life.

The years rolled slowly along with third grade becoming fourth grade, fourth grade becoming fifth grade and in June of 1976, I graduated elementary school. Little did I know of the monumental changes and challenges that were in store for me.

I entered sixth grade (Junior High School) that fall to experience a rude awakening. Gone was the intimacy of a single teacher in a single classroom. The school seemed gigantic. It had long halls with rows of lockers and there were students *everywhere*. There were couples walking around holding hands, arm and arm and some were even kissing!!! Some of the older students were smoking cigarettes in the bathroom and there was talk about parties and alcohol, "joints" and "doobies" and I don't mean the Doobie Brothers. All of a sudden the people you talked to and hung around with; the type of music you listened to, your hairstyle and the kind of clothes you wore *mattered immensely*. Everything seemed to be about image. If you could show something off, you'd show it off and if you had something to brag about, you'd brag about it. If you weren't naturally cool, you had to at least pretend that you were. Being the shy, insecure kid, I felt totally overwhelmed and completely shell-shocked.

It took a few months of getting used to, but in time I did settle in and began to get a feel for my new environment. It didn't take me long to figure out that a class system existed among the student body. You had three distinct groups: jocks, greasers and nerds. Coming from my background (most of my mother's brothers were serious athletes), the clean-cut and popular jocks would be the group that appealed to me most and direction I would take, for now. Izod shirts, Levi pants and Nike sneakers became an absolute "must have" and to complete my makeover, I joined the track team. My new image was almost intact. The only thing left was my music.

On October 29, 1976, the New York glam rock group Kiss appeared and performed (lip-synched) on the Paul Lynne Halloween television special. Much like the influence The Beatles on the Ed Sullivan Show had on the generation before; this event had an enormous impact on me, and most likely the thousands of other kids watching the program that night. I recall being spellbound by the combination of high-energy rock and roll music coupled with this larger-than-life super hero comic book image. For a long time, Kiss would become *my* band and my obsession. Kiss wasn't just a band I loved; it also gave me some degree of credibility for in 1976/77, it was cool to like Kiss.

Discovering rock music was an exciting time in my life and it would forever changed my life but it also marked the beginning of what would become a strained relationship with my parents, particularly my mother.

Them Changes

I was in the seventh grade when an incident took place that would change my life in school for years to come: bullying. Bullies have the uncanny ability, like any predator, to seek out the weak and timid and pounce and that's exactly what happened to me on that fateful day. I was walking through the library when a classmate, out of nowhere and completely unprovoked, started pushing me around. I was shocked and stunned and unfortunately did nothing to retaliate. If I simply stood my ground most likely he would have backed off and that would have been the end of it, but instead, I wilted. To make matters worse, the following day I made the fatal mistake of offering him part of my lunch. It was right then and there that the floodgates of bullying became wide opened and for the next three years I become what amounted to his in school servant. Refusing to go to my parents or teachers for fear of looking weak, I painfully and begrudgingly accept this role. Fear, humiliation, and intimidation would become the feelings that would dominate the rest of my time in junior high school and beyond.

Other aspects of my life were changing around this time as well. Starting in junior high, 1970's arena rock music, and Kiss in particular, became my new passion and were quickly beginning to replace modeling and playing army as my favorite past times. Queen, Led Zeppelin, Aerosmith, ZZ Top and Cheap Trick were just a few of my many favorite groups and I would spend endless hours listening to their records, studying the cover art and pouring over the lyrics and liner notes. Saturday mornings now were typically spent going to breakfast with my dad and then to a local record store. There, he would purchase jazz records for himself and buy one or two rock albums for me and I was beginning to amass quite a record collection. Saturday *nights* on the other hand were an altogether different story.

When fantasy play no longer provided for me a satisfactory form of entertainment; video game arcades, hanging out and getting into trouble did. I was spending more and more time away from home and with that my need for addition funds became apparent. When my measly allowance would no longer suffice, I began mowing lawns in the summer and shoveling driveways in the winter to generate additional income. There was also the occasional dip into my mom's pocketbook or dad's wallet. For fun, my friends and I would engage in snowballing cars, egg houses and petty vandalism. I loved the adrenaline high that came from being chased by an angry motorist or police officer. Another form of getting "high" would be just around the corner.

I began my final year of junior high school during the fall of 1978 dealing with the same bully intimidation that had begun the year before. It was a feeling that hung over my head like a dark cloud, which I did my best to cover up. Eventually this pressure reached critical mass and with encouragement from my father, I decided to fight back. The battle would take place after school at a local cemetery. When we finally got there, after a very long and tense bus ride, and were face to face, nothing happened. No matter how hard I tried or how much I wanted to, I could not bring myself to fight him. As much as I didn't want to experience the physical pain of fighting, it disgusted me *more* to actual inflict physical pain onto another person. This was a major disappointment and setback because I wanted so badly to break free from this twisted relationship. But for the time being, it would be back to bullying business as usual. My freedom would still be a couple of years away.

My entering senior high school in September of 1979 brought more changes. One of them was my first experience with alcohol. An uncle of mine had a food catering business and often times my mother, my sister and I would help with cleaning up after functions for extra money. Going into work one night, I noticed that there were small cups of white wine, some full and some half empty, left on the dinner tables. During clean up, and behind my mother's back, I started guzzling down all this left over wine. By the end of work I was feeling pretty tipsy and very silly and I remember thinking to myself; this feels pretty neat. It would be a feeling that I would continue to chase for quite some time.

Now that I was a freshman in high school, I started feeling that it was time for another makeover and one that presented a harder and tougher image. Mostly influenced by the rock music I was so enamored by, the clean-cut preppie jock persona I had recently embraced no longer appealed to me. I started to grow my hair out. I wore rock concert T-shirts in place of the Izod ones, my crisp corduroys became torn and battered blue jeans and my Nike sneakers became untied Dexter hiking boots. With my chain wallet, gray hoodie and black leather jacket I became the bad boy rebel rock and roller. Due to my lack of interest in school, my grades began to go steadily downhill and I was once again, spending less and less time at home. My mother and father were, needless to say, concerned and probably for good reason but there was no turning back for me. The times they certainly were a changin'.

Although I was still painfully shy around girls I did manage to land my first girlfriend during the summer of 1980. The relationship was rather short lived for I didn't have near what it would have taken to keep her. Nonetheless she was beautiful and fun to be around and I was just happy to be in her presence. And I remember clearly my father's first and only advice about sex: "Keep your pecker in your pants." It was funny, because at that time, engaging in sexual relations didn't matter to me. I was very much content to satisfy myself sexually. Besides, it was safe, easy and no one got hurt.*

*Sex and sexuality can an awkward, embarrassing and somewhat uncomfortable subject and I was torn between whether or not I should talk about sex in this revised edition of my book for fear that it might take away from the book's primary objective: helping people discover God. But because sex is a natural, normal and *significant* part of the human experience, I feel it that should not be ignored. Besides being one of life's great *physical* pleasures, it can also be an expression of love, unity and devotion. It's how couples *connect* and how human beings are *created*. But as wonderful and beautiful as sex can be, there are a great many problems and challenges associated with it. Sex can elicit some of the most heart wrenching emotions such as betrayal, jealousy, rejection and inadequacy. It has also been the ruin of many a good person. Moreover sex can bring about Child Abuse, Unwanted Pregnancy, Abortion, Sexual Transmitted Diseases, Pedophilia, Prostitution, Adultery, Rape, Etc . . . There is also the Emotional Pain and Sorrow it can cause when someone is being used simply for sex. These are all very, very serious issues that face this world which is why sex is so controversial; why it is often seen as dirty and why it is scorned and looked down upon. But if we are sensitive, responsible, intelligent, educated, wise, cautious, disciplined, strong willed, safe and even *spiritual* about sex, all of the heartbreak and tragedy associated with sex *could be eliminated*. Often times, it's not the object or activity (sex, guns, money, food, gambling, etc . . .) that's the problem but the way in which it is used or too often times, *misused*.

By the time I started my sophomore year in high school, the bully's grip on my life was gradually loosening. We both had this "bad boy" image in common and started to become real friends. We would smoke cigarettes, listen to southern rock music and talk about girls and driving fast cars. We even got a job together washing dishes and at a local hotel. It was also during this period in my life that I started to experiment with marijuana.

Smoking marijuana was something that immediately appealed to me for several reasons. First because it took away the shyness and insecurity I had around people, especially girls. Secondly, it seemed to enhance the things I was doing most at that time which were playing arcade games, listening to music and going to parties. And lastly, it fit perfectly with the bad boy image I was trying to cultivate. Besides that, smoking "pot" was bad, cool, hip and fashionable.

By 1981 I had completely embraced, much to my parents chagrin, my new image and lifestyle. By that time, rock groups like Kiss (who made the grave mistake of going first to disco then to pop) had fallen out of favor with most hard rock fans like myself and were being replaced by tougher "Heavy Metal" groups. Bands like AC/DC, Black Sabbath, Iron Maiden and Judas Priest were the movement's key representatives and I ate them all up hook, line and sinker. The music was loud, tough, macho and aggressive. Loaded with volume, attitude, ego and testosterone it fit perfectly with the person I had become: rebellious and defiant. It was funny and somewhat ironic because while I was someone who wanted to *present* this tough

image, I was truly anything but. Deep down, I was
a pushover. All I really wanted to do was have fun,
get along with others and avoid anything that had
to do with violence.

My home life by this time, as you might have
imagined, had become pretty cantankerous. By the
early 1980's, most of the domestic shoe industry
had moved overseas (the Orient) and my father
had gone with it. This basically left my mother
to parent me alone and I took complete advantage
of it. School became nothing more than a social
club and my grades reflected this, which caused
me (much to my delight) to repeat my sophomore
year. I was smoking marijuana *several* times a day
and doing harder drugs on the weekends. From
my vantage point, life was fantastic but in reality
it couldn't have been much worse.

During the fall of 1981, my daily ritual of
smoking marijuana before school finally caught up
with me and I was given a twenty day out of school
suspension or "vacation" as I viewed it. Although
the time away from school didn't bother me, what
did bother me was the fact that everybody on
the other side of the cultural fence (grown-ups)

now knew what I was doing. I had let down my parents, teachers, neighbors, aunt and uncles, my mother's friends and many others. I felt ashamed, embarrassed and humiliated but my shame didn't last very long. Later that same school year, I was caught smoking on the bus on the way to school and this time, I was expelled. In order to be reinstated, I had to go before the school board with my parents and plead my case. The board allowed me to return to school to further my education and change my ways, which I did, for a time.

I managed to finish the school year somewhat successfully (I passed) and began working on getting my drivers license. After receiving the coveted prize I spent the summer tooling around town in my 1972 Volkswagon Beetle and falling in love with a fifteen-year-old brunette from Haverhill, Massachusetts. We began a plutonic relationship that fall that lasted a whole six months. We had a lot of fun together and truly enjoyed each other's company. The fact that we didn't engage in sex was fine with me because once again, I was content to take care of that urge by myself and more importantly, I could avoid the pitfalls that often occur with immature sexual activity. Besides

I was pretty adept at fabricating stories about how great our love life was. As long as it looked good and sounded good to my peers, I was happy.

During the winter of 1983 my rock and roll fantasy became a reality when I purchased my first instrument: a used set of drums. With just a few days of practice under my belt I assembled a band that would rehearse in the basement of my family's home. Just imagine for a moment my mother (Dad's working full-time in China) sitting quietly at the kitchen table reading the newspaper and sipping a cup of coffee while a large contingent of funky looking people (band and various on-lookers) come rolling though the house like a freight train carry a truckload of guitars and amplifiers down to my basement/bedroom practice space. My mother tried to be a good sport but could only tolerate the loud noise for so long. She finally put an end to this calamity by changing the locks on all the doors of our house. But by then it was too late for I had been bitten by the performing bug and would continue playing music, in some capacity, for the rest of my life.

During the spring of my junior year in high school, I had my first real sexual experience. She was sweet, pretty and experienced and there was a great deal of risk involved with this relationship mainly in the form of an extremely jealous boyfriend. I never should have traveled down that road but I was infatuated and too selfish at that time to have considered the feelings of anyone else other than myself. The relationship came to an abrupt end when the person she had been previously involved with found out about our liaison due to my loose lips (bragging) and I miraculously escaped serious bodily injury. It was a hard lesson, but one that could have been a lot harder. Unfortunately sex at that time, personally speaking, was more about impressing friends and ego-tripping as opposed to making an honest, heartfelt connection with someone you really cared about.

The fall and winter months of my senior year in high school were pretty uneventful. It was the same ole, same ole. I was working part time washing dishes at a local country club, playing drums with my garage band, listening to records, smoking pot and drinking alcohol with my good time buddies and trying to get away with doing as little as possible in school. Little did I know that right around the corner, an event would take place that would change the course of my life forever.

Finding God (My Discovery)

During the fall of 1983 I met a gentleman who was working at a local gas station. He had come of age during the 1960's and was a record collector and rock drummer. We hit it off immediately and quickly became good friends. I would spend many nights the gas station where we'd smoke cigarettes and talk endlessly about playing drums, 60's psychedelic rock music and Boston Celtics basketball. But it was during a warm spring evening in May of 1984 when the conversation veered of the normal beaten path.

It was a night like any other talking with my buddy at the gas station, when the conversation turned from typical to spiritual prompted by the presence of a rather large blue book lying on the table in front of us. My friend had known God for quite some time and encouraged by my questions, began to share with me his knowledge

and experiences regarding God and religion. As
the conversation grew deeper, I could feel my soul
begin to stir with the wonder and excitement that
spiritual truth can elicit. We talked for hours that
night about God and I just knew to the depths of
my soul that the words he spoke to me that evening
were *true* and it was a conversation I will always
remember.

On the drive home that night, I thought
intensely about our talk and about how much I
wanted to delve deeper into the truths we had
discussed and as I drove I could fell my soul
stirring with an incredible sense of anticipation.
When I arrived home, I immediately went to my
room and began the process of trying to experience
this incredible truth (God) for myself. I started
by shutting off all the lights and soon after was
lying face up flat on my bed. As I laid there in the
silent darkness I began to think about the truths
that were spoken to me earlier that evening. Then
I began to talk to God. I expressed to Him how
much I wanted to know Him and if He was really
with me and did He truly love me unconditionally.
Were all these things true? And as I opened my
mind to Him I could fell my heart begin overflow

with pure, unabashed love that was coming directly from God's Spirit Presence *within me*. Tears of joy and bliss washed down my face in torrents and I just lied there basking in the glow of God's embrace, bathing in His love light for what seemed like hours, just the two of us. For that time, I felt like I was the only person on earth and God's only child. It was and still remains to this day one of the most special, powerful, enlightening, and monumental events I have ever experienced. This was my baptism and the night God and I become partners: together forever in holy matrimony.

When the thrill of that evening began to subside a few days later, it gave me a chance to evaluate, in the light of day, just what happened to me on that fateful night. And I clearly remember being shocked by the *magnitude* of it all. This was not some dream, fantasy or drug induced illusion. This was not wishful thinking or blind acceptance. It was not a figment of my imagination or a desperate need for something greater to believe in: of a "higher power." It was not some new found "state of mind" or a new belief in some distant hope. *Who* I found that evening and *what* I experienced went far, far beyond my previous belief in the idea or *concept* of a God. This event took me all the way to the *actual realization*, much to my astonishment, that God was not only a real living *Being* (a *Someone* not a *something*) but also that He truly was *present within me*! This was absolutely stunning to someone who never really thought about connecting with God on quite this level. In a matter of a few short hours, I (an 18 year old kid and hardly the cream of intelligentsia) had reached the *pinnacle of spiritual discovery*! From that day forward God was no longer an unsure belief in my mind but an *absolute reality* that resided there. And to now realize the difference between what was once a hazy belief and now a concrete reality was, in a word, *Colossal*.

AFTER GOD

Rebirth

Once the euphoria and elation of my personal epiphany/revelation subsided, I settle back into life as usual but with one major and profound difference: I knew now without a stitch of doubt that I had God's Living Presence within me. I became, in a sense, born again and from this point forward, it would longer be simply me alone in life: it would be *us*. And although it would take many years for my relationship with God to fully blossom, it initially provided me with some much-needed *drive* for a much-needed change in *direction*.

In June, I graduated high school with little to celebrate and with no idea as to what I wanted to do with my life as far as a career was concerned. I was in poor health smoking a pack of cigarettes a day, getting little in the way of exercise and a living on a diet consisting of mainly cheap fast food. Drug and alcohol use were at their peak and so was my penchant for doing as little as possible. Finding God did not magically change my attitude and behavior (soul) overnight but it did mark the *beginning* of what would eventually become the complete end of my destructive, excessive and self-abusive lifestyle. It was also critical in helping me to navigate my way though the uncharted waters of change that were soon to be rushing by my front doorstep. I don't know where I would have ended up or what kind of life I would have lead had I not made this discovery but I am *absolutely positive* it would not be anything close to the life I live today.

In addition to feeling elated about finding God, I also felt a degree of awkwardness and even embarrassment. After some tense and uncomfortable encounters with family and friends, who thought, "this boy must be delusional," I began to realize I had not the wisdom and experience to accurately describe to others just what happened to me that night I found God. I found it especially difficult explaining to people that I had discovered God without the aid of religion or other traditional forms of spiritual inspiration. People would ask me, "Well, *what* are you?" I didn't know what to say initially. But after thinking about it, I would just tell them that I simply found God. I had no idea what to call myself other than a person who had found God. I also started to feel somewhat embarrassed to even admit to people that I had anything to do with God for fear they would have the same preconceived notions that even I had about people who were religious or spiritual. I was afraid that people would think that I now thought of myself as better or in some way superior to them, or that all of sudden they would have to start minding their P's and Q's around me, or that I would in some way try to pressure or coerce then into joining some group or organization. I very quickly found myself becoming more and more reticent when it came to opening up to people about my newfound spirituality. It would take many years for me to acquire a greater understanding of the God experience and with it a more effective way of expressing it.

1985—The Lost Year

Life after high school was somewhat of a rude awakening. Gone were the dozens of friends I'd see everyday at school. Gone were the six-hour workdays and the years with five weeks vacation time with summers off. My life as a slacker would have to come to an end. It was now time to think about growing up and what direction I would be taking which I wasn't exactly thrilled about doing. In October, I got a full-time job (the thought of furthering my education was at this time, out of the question) as a plastics extruder operator. Although the hours were tough (3 p.m. to 11:30 p.m.) and the work was laborious, it was a good wakeup call as to what the real, blue collar working world was all about.

By spring I could feel myself becoming nervous and uneasy about my future. And although I had found a better job packaging computer terminals, I felt like my life was going nowhere fast. Many of my friends were going off in different directions, which left me feeling extremely lonely at times. Plus, I wanted desperately to meet a girl who I could form a more serious and long-term relationship with. I was also plagued by the same bad habits I developed in high school causing my home life to become more and more stressful. My mother had grown sick and tired of my ways and was pressuring me hard to go back to school, get an education and find a "real" job. As an alternative, and also for my earlier love for the military, I began, with a good friend of mine, to look into joining one of the armed forces. Besides, I really had nothing to lose.

In April, my friend and I walked into the local recruiting office to inquire about life in the Army as well as a program called the "buddy system." After spending an hour or so with the Sergeant, we left the facility feeling excited, optimistic and raring to go. My mother, much to my surprise, was against it but my father, as you might imagine, was all for it. If I could have joined the Army that afternoon I would have done it but as the weeks passed my enthusiasm waned, and by the time we were supposed to be sworn in, I backed out. After some serious soul searching coupled with some advice from others, I came to the realization that life in a military probably wasn't for me. My buddy on the other hand, ended up going through with it and was the best thing that could have happened to him at that time. Feeling relieved, I resumed my job at the computer company and it was back to business as usual.

That summer, I found myself going through yet another image and style transformation. I was 20 years old, the year 1985 and new T.V. series called "Miami Vice" was changing way I now looked (and probably many other guys) at fashion and style. I soon replaced my ripped jeans, hiking boots and leather jacket with a white sports coat, pink chinos and tan loafers. I even cut my hair, which was unimaginable just 6 months earlier. I sold my Volkswagen Beetle for a BMW 320i and my drugs of choice became cocaine and wine coolers. My taste in music also changed. I found myself listening less to the "childish" rough and tumble heavy metal music of my teen years and more to the digital pop and dance music of bands like Wham, Duran Duran and Mr. Mister. Everything on the outside looked fabulous but on the inside so much was missing and deep down, I knew it.

I continued to work through that summer but in the fall was laid off. I quickly found employment at a printed circuit company and began working in the shipping department. From shipping I slowly made the transition to delivery driver and found myself really taking a liking this new position. It allowed me freedom of movement without anyone looking over my shoulder. It gave to time to think and daydream. I could also listen to news or music on the radio. Most importantly it gave me the opportunity to see new places and meet new people.

New Year's Eve saw me take another step towards self-improvement (my prior resolution was to quit smoking cigarettes), which was to start exercising and with that suspend my marijuana use.

That February of 1986, while I was doing some chores in the packaging department at work, a conversation with some co-workers started to get spiritual. There was one woman in particular who seemed to be very religious and also very passionate about it. The exchanged turned into a rather heated debate about the nature of God, specifically God's wrath, anger, and vengeance. She was very calm, confident and resolute about her argument justifying how bad people deserve God's wrath and extreme punishment. I felt enraged and incensed thinking to myself, that's not the God I know but there was little I could say because at that time I sorely lacked the spiritual insight and life experience to offer a clear and accurate rebuttal. It had been a few months shy of two years since I had discovered God and in that time was doing very little to develop an ongoing intimate connection with Him. I walked away feeling dejected and defeated but the experience was valuable in that it prompted me to seek out my old friend and mentor from the gas station who had been so instrumental in helping me with my initial spiritual awakening.

Reconnecting

The very next day I knocked on the door of the house where my old friend and his family were living. We hadn't spoken to each other in over a year so we spent the next few hours just talking and getting reacquainted with each other. It was great to reconnect with him for I truly missed him and the friendship we once shared. After the frustrating conversation with my co-worker the day before, I was feeling a bit lost spiritual speaking and needed some kind of a kick in the pants to get me thinking about God again. That visit and conversation became the jump-start that I so desperately needed in order for me to really get *moving* spiritually and start building a more substantial relationship with God. And not to mention, re-igniting what was once a very important and meaningful friendship.

It's not that I ever lost God, it's just that I had lost my way spiritually which caused a degree of stagnation that ultimately lead to some significant regression in regards to my developing soul. It was now time for me to take my initial discovery into the full-time, full-blown active intimate relationship that I was feeling it could be.

Remember that large blue book I mentioned earlier? It was the book that I first saw on the table at the gas station the night I found God. Well, my friend had been, and still is to this day, an avid reader and studier of this great book. It is a 3 inch thick, 2000 plus page document that explains in great detail many subjects but primarily God, our universe, planet earth and the life and teachings of Jesus. It is in a word, *incredible*. It's been called a revelation. I believe that it is.

After talking about it with my friend, I found myself wanting to know more about this mysterious document. This was perfect because on Sunday mornings, a small group of inquiring minds (which now would include myself) would gather at my friend's house to read a segment of the book then engage in an open discussion about the subject matter that was just read. The meetings were always stimulating. And not only did they help me expand and broaden my thinking, but they also brought me into contact with like-minded individuals who were looking to become better people and understand the greater universe around them.

Besides God, my friend and I had many things in common. When we weren't discussing things spiritual, we'd often listen to music from his impressing record library, or hang out together watching Boston sports (1986 was a great year for that) or talk about drums and drummers which both of us were very passionate about. Those were great times and we remain the best of friends to this day.

Once again, my life at home, living with my parents, was shaky at best. Although I was working a full time job, there was subtle pressure from my parents to further my education in hopes of finding/getting an actual "career." My mother would constantly tell me, "You just can't go on living at home working menial jobs." She would have to patient with me for I was still unsure of what I wanted to do with my life long-term. For the time being, I was content to go to work, get my paycheck, hang out with friends, buy records, play drums and hopefully meet a girl I could actually fall in love with.

That summer, I took a week's vacation and flew out to Beaverton, Oregon to visit my father who was living and working there. He had taken a job for a large shoe company that was based there and suggested I move out there, live with him and maybe he could get me a job working for them. It seemed like a good idea and besides, the area was beautiful, the people seemed nice and I had very little (other than a few close friends and family, which isn't little) to lose. I was going nowhere with my present job, my prospects for love seemed hopeless and my home life was becoming unbearable. After thinking about it all that summer, I decided it was time for me to take a chance and make a new start.

Go West Young Man

That fall I laid the groundwork for what would be my first experience away from home. I had heard that friend of mine was also looking to make a move out west so I contacted him to inquire about taking the trip together. Not only would this provide me with a travel companion but also it would help defray the costs of travel. After getting in touch with him, he agreed it would be beneficial for the both us so we set a date and started packing. We departed New England on October 28, 1986 (The day after the Boston Red Sox lost the 1986 World Series to the New York Mets) and headed west. Just to see the country at ground level was exciting and fun. It felt mature to be away from home, eating out and staying at hotels. After four days of traveling, we arrived in Los Angeles where I my friend would be living. After spending one night, I departed the next morning with the thought of seeing as much of the California coast as possible. The drive up the coast was simply beautiful. There were mountains to my right and the sparkling blue waters of the Pacific Ocean to my left. I would made frequent stops to stand at the edge of magnificent cliffs with crashing waves a hundred feet below and it would literally take your breath away. I recall thinking: sometimes the line between life and death is only a few inches.

I spent the first night of my west coast trip in Sacramento. I arrived late and left early so I didn't get to see much of the state's capitol. What I remember most about the ride north on Interstate 5 was the Shasta National Forest. What natural beauty. I arrived in Beaverton, Oregon later that night and immediately moved into the house my parents (mom had arrived a week or so earlier) were temporarily living in. It was certainly weird living in a strange home in a new area knowing only a handful of people but after a few days, I began to adjust to these new surroundings.

Shortly after my arrival in Oregon, the shoe company my father was working for had implemented a hiring freeze and was in the process of moving most of it's manufacturing overseas so any chance of my getting a job there quickly evaporated. Even my dad was given the choice of either moving to Bangkok, Thailand or risk being laid off. It was an easy decision for my father because he had already spent a considerable amount of time in the Orient and really enjoyed living and working there. After assuring my father I would be fine on my own, he accepted the offer and would soon be on his way. Before they left, my parents set me up in a really nice apartment just a few minutes from the center of town. With everything now in place, my dad left for Thailand and my mother went back home to New England and for the first time in my life, I was completely on my own.

After settling into my new place, I found employment at a local high tech company, which were abundant during the late 1980's. I met some very nice people there who after realizing I was new to the area, took me into their hearts and homes. Although they did their best to make me feel a part of the community I couldn't help feeling a bit detached as well as lonely and homesick. But instead of dwelling on it, I decided to take action.

I had been thinking about a possible career in drafting so that winter, I enrolled at Portland Community College taking a class in technical drawing. Besides education, it was another way to meet new people, especially the opposite sex. In addition to my going to school, I joined a local gym in an effort to change my appearance and more importantly, increase my odds of acquiring a girlfriend. I may not have been able to change my big nose or my kinky hair, but I could change my physique. Lifting weights, supplements and strict dieting became an *obsession* that would continue for years to come.

My life here in Oregon was moving along nicely. I had a job that I enjoyed and my nights were spent either at school or working out at the gym. Weekends usually consisted of shopping at used record stores in downtown Portland. Fortunately, I made some friends who really helped me adjust to a rather challenging time but something big was still missing. I had yet to find that special someone I so desperately longed for.

As winter became spring, the possibilities of my staying in Oregon for any real length of time were diminishing. I had no roots there, no family there, and no history there. I didn't have one deep friendship. I was single and painfully lonely. Even my relationship with God couldn't fill the void I was feeling most everyday. I greatly missed my home and family, my few good friends and those inspiring Sunday meetings. My time in Oregon had been valuable for it taught me how to be independent and responsible for myself and this in turn gave me a sense of pride and self-esteem. But in the end my loneliness and homesickness got the best of me and by early summer I made the decision to go back home to New England and start all over again.

That June, a good friend of mine from back home flew out to Oregon to hang out with me for a few days but he was there primarily to take the long road trip back to New Hampshire. We left two days after the Boston Celtics lost to the Los Angeles Lakers in the 1987 NBA finals. The drive home was a lot of fun but during those long hours behind the steering wheel all I could think about was, "Now what are you going to do?"

Starting Over

When I arrived back home, I quickly re-connected with all of my good friends and family. It was good to get home to family and also feel that sense of *community* that I never really experienced in Oregon. I took that entire summer off trying to put off the inevitable: my future. The options were simple, either get a full-time job or get back to school. After weighing my choices, I decided to enroll at an area technical college with hopes of getting a degree in computer-aided drafting or CAD. This for well for me in two ways: One, I thought it might be a job I could perform well and *enjoy*, and secondly and more importantly, it would keep my parents, especially my mother, off my back.

The next year and a half of my life was spent going to school full-time and working part-time. I struggled with many of my classes with the exception of psychology, which I found fascinating. Due to my natural interest in psych, I probably should have changed my ambitions immediately right then and there but because of my lack of confidence and self-awareness, failed to do so. But for the time being I would continue on my present path at school and work my tolerable part-time job all the while obsessing over my appearance. I had yet to find that special someone and because of that was becoming more and more depressed. And when you're (personally speaking) twenty something, single, celibate and living with your mom, you start to think there's something seriously wrong with you. By and large I was one very unhappy individual. Fortunately I had a small but solid support system (made up of a few good friends), which also included God, who I was now beginning to lean on more and more. This support network was *critical* to me and is what would pull me through these rather difficult and strenuous times.

For the New Year, I quit drinking alcohol (which I did very little of) and in February I made the monumental decision to drop out of college. The more time I spent learning about CAD (computer aided design) the more I realized it wasn't what I wanted to do for a career. As you might imagine, this went over like a lead balloon with my parents, especially my mother who basically hit the roof.

I will never forget the conversation that night. It was a no holds barred debate that allowed us both to, once and for all, clear the air and speak our minds without fear or apprehension. It was also a conversation where no one walked away feeling particularly good about what was spoken but still was very important to have at that point in time. I could understand my mother's concern, but at the same time I had to remind her that it was *my life* and not hers and that *I* had to be happy with the direction I was taking or else risk becoming an unhappy, unfulfilled person which I basically was. It was painful as anything because the last thing I (or most anyone) wanted to do is disappoint my parents. For years I had this "what are you going to do with your life" monkey on my back and now it was time for me to shed that burden, find myself and finally start being *true to myself*. Dropping out of college was a watershed event in my life because it allowed me to put myself squarely on the path (artistically and spiritually) that I am still on today.

My first order of business was to get back into playing the drums. As time passed and the more I thought about it, the more I realized that I am simply a person who is cut from an artist's cloth thanks in large part to my father's side of the family. It's who I am and what I am. Unfortunately, this was a reality that my mother simply could not embrace or accept. But because music and art were the things I was most passionate about, it only made sense that I should pursue a career within those realms. I immediately bought a set of drums from a musician friend of mine having sold my original kit when I moved out west. I also rented a shed from this same friend and starting studying and practicing my instrument with a purpose. I even started taking drum lessons at a local music store but those didn't last very long because, once again, I preferred learning on my known terms and at my own tempo (no pun intended).

My other goal at this time was to deepen my relationship with God. This was critical for me in light of all the changes I was going though. Especially the tension I was feeling with my mother. I would accomplish this in a personal way with individual prayer and worship and socially during our Sunday morning study meetings. I had been bodybuilding for quite some time but it was high time that I start doing some serious *soul* building.

That fall, I signed up for classes at a local community college that specialized in liberal arts but this time, it would be for subjects that *I* wanted to study: Art and Music. The other fall study on my agenda would be to read from cover to cover all 2097 pages of the book that was the subject of our Sunday morning study group. Everyday after my classes I would go straight to the school library to read from this book for one full hour. I was feeling really good about the progress I was making in my life with the exception of two areas: my life at home and the fact that I was still single.

Life at home, since I dropped out of Technical College, was becoming increasingly tense and was fast reaching the point of being intolerable. My mother was not at all happy with the direction my life was going in and let me know this on an almost daily basis. It was getting to the point where I could no longer take it and I knew something would have to give. And since my parents weren't going anywhere it was becoming painfully obvious that I had to leave home and fast.

Freedom Sweet Freedom

In November, I got the opportunity to rent a small house that was owned by a good friend of mines mother in a neighboring town not far from our family home for a whopping three hundred dollars a month. It was just what the doctor ordered. The best thing about this house was that I could play my drums there, which was one of the few gratifying things I had going on in my life at that time. With great fervor and determination I began to reshape and refresh the interior of this rather small dwelling, which was in pretty rough shape due to the previous occupants, to create my new personal, holy sanctuary. After a little money and a whole lot of blood, sweat and tears, I created a home that reflected who I was. There was impressionistic art on the walls, a good amount of vinyl records, my stereo, an exercise machine and my drums. Oh yeah, it also had a bathroom and a place to eat. It would be a new decade of freedom, independence, self-reliance and hopefully, greater *happiness*. I would officially move in on New Year's Day, January 1, 1990.

I began this new decade with a great deal of optimism. I was not using marijuana at this time, as it was my New Year's resolution not to do for a while and as a result, my mind was sharp, clear and focused. And as hard as it was to be alone (still no girlfriend) on this new journey, I was free and independent to pursue what I believed was my destiny, which was to be an artist/musician. I knew it would be hard and I knew I'd probably be hungry but it was the one thing besides God that I was passionate and serious about. This would be a time of determination and discipline and I was ready for it. My daily routine was strict and as follows;

8:00 a.m. to 8:30—Breakfast
8:30 a.m. to 10:00—Book Study
10:00 a.m. to 12:00 noon—Drum Practice
12:00 p.m. to 12:30—Lunch Break
12:30 p.m. to 3:30—Drum Practice
3:45 p.m. to 8:30 p.m.—Work
9:00 p.m. to 10:00—Exercise, Prayer and Worship

My daily routine, difficult as it was at times, was yielding some real nutritious fruit. My relationship *with* God and my understanding *of*

God was grower deeper and deeper by the day. I was feeling healthier physically and my proficiency as a drummer was becoming greater. As my mind and thinking was expanding so too were my ears. The heavy metal and pop music of 1980's had run their course for me as well as millions of other listeners but instead of turning to the newer sounds of "grunge" rock, I discovered the beauty and emotion of 1960's jazz, folk and blues music. They became my "alternative" music and with what little extra money I had, I would scour used record stores trying to obtain vintage vinyl L.P.'s that were fairly plentiful at that time due to the advent of the Compact Disc. I had my little home, my drums and my records, God and one or two close friends. It was a very lonely period in my live but also a very constructive one.

The absence of a soul mate in my life left a hole in my being that no one else (not even God) was capable of filling. Not a single day went by that I wasn't thinking about finding her. Over the years, I had several opportunities to engage in relationships with women, even sexual relations. But as tempting as it might have been and as sexually charged as I was at that time, unless the girl was someone I could see myself with *long term*, sex was out of the question. I could not bring myself to take advantage of a girl, (especially in light of my recent spiritual growth) who I didn't have real and deep feelings for and besides in my mind, sex = commitment. At this point in my life, it would be all or nothing at all.

In April, I was laid off from my part time job and forced to look for work. After painting my parent's home, I began pounding the pavement in search of permanent full time employment. After scuffing for a few weeks, I walked into a local, family owned and operated, automotive supply store to see if they needed any driver help. Thinking back to my driving days at the printed circuit board company, this would be something I could see myself doing long term. As fate would have it, they needed someone to fill that position and I was quickly hired as a full time delivery driver. Little did I know at the time that this would be a job I would keep to this day and would lead to an event that would *completely* change my life.

I quickly settled into my new driving job, which was perfect for the unskilled, uneducated "artist" that I was/am. It was rather simple and relatively stress free which allowed me ample time to think, dream and fantasize. And I could also listen to the radio (mainly Boston sports talk and NPR) but most importantly it gave me the opportunity to meet a wealth of new and interesting people. I also developed a strong friendship with one of my co-workers Scott, who happened to be the owner's grandson. After work, we would take out his boat and go fishing or tubing or go to my place, get high and listen to the blues, which was his favorite genre of music. Over time we became the best of friends and still are even to this day.

Things had been going great that summer when out of the blue tragedy struck. My father, who was working overseas as a shoe consultant, fainted due to his blood sugar level and severely hit his head. The blow struck a steel plate in his skull that was surgically placed there as a result of injuries sustained in the war. He quickly lapsed into a coma. My mother, sister and I had a family meeting to discuss what our options were and what needed to be done. I remember expressing to my mother and that we should "let him go" (take him off life-support) while he was still in Thailand.

My reasoning was that if his soul had departed his body and has moved on, then there is no need to keep his physical body alive. And if his soul had not departed, we would be keeping his conscious mind a prisoner trapped in his paralyzed body much like the soldier in the 1971 film, "Johnny Got His Gun" that depicts a WWI soldier whose conscious/thinking mind is trapped within his paralyzed body. I somehow envisioned that this would become my father's fate for years to come and it broke my heart. I knew God and within that relationship was completely confident that his life would be everlasting and that by letting him go, my father would be free from his infirmities. But it was ultimately my mother's decision and she along with my sister, decided that someone should fly out to Thailand and bring him back to the states where he would hopefully make a full recovery. There were many reasons why my mother could not bring herself to release my father from this world and it would take sometime for me to understand the reasons why.

After the decision was made to bring him home, my brother (from my father's first marriage in 1946) volunteered to fly out to Thailand and bring my father home. Upon returning home, my father was admitted into an area VA hospital and placed on life support. This is where he would spend the remained of his life.

Love at First Night

On a Friday night in late September, Scott dropped by my little house to show me a purchase he had just made. With him were his long time girl friend, Carolyn and her sister Katherine. They only stayed a short while and I thought little of it but we made plans to get together, all four of us the following night for dinner.

It was a casual get together not intended to be any kind of a "set up" although Carolyn thought I should meet her sister thinking we would have quite a bit in common. Little did she know. As the night progressed and we had the chance to get acquainted, we both started to realize how much we really did have in common. But it wasn't just the casual, we both like chocolate commonalities, it was the *deeper, core* values that we shared and how we both felt about *serious* issues that made our meeting so compelling and intriguing. Now that's not to say I wasn't physically attracted to her because I most definitely was, but this went far beyond that. It was her depth and beauty from *within* that made her so attractive to me and unlike any woman I had ever met in my life. And to top it all off, she spiritually minded as well! That night, something very *real* was happening between us and we both knew it but there was one problem: she already had a significant other.

When I got home that night, all I could think about was this amazing woman. She was beautiful, kind, thoughtful and intelligent but the fact that she had a long time boyfriend made her absolutely *off limits*. I was reminded of my earlier experience of seeing someone who was involve with someone else and all the trouble that had caused so there was *no way* I was going down that road again and I am sure she wouldn't have either. Besides that, it was just morally wrong.

This same quartet got together a few days later to hang out and again there was an undeniable chemistry between us. At one point in the evening, our eyes briefly met and we smiled and quickly looked the other way. Once again I would have to ignore my thoughts and feelings.

A week or so later I heard a knock at my door and it was Katherine. She wanted to know if would be willing to make her a "mix tape" from my vinyl record collection and I enthusiastically replied, "Sure, we can work on it together." She came over to my little house later that day and we began to select songs to record. It was a lot of fun. But it also gave us a chance to talk about a wide range of topics. One of the subjects we discussed in depth was the relationship with her boyfriend and how it had been slowly disintegrating for quite sometime and how she really didn't know how to end it. All I could say to her was, "follow your heart" and trust where it takes you hoping all the while that it would lead her straight to me.

The next time I talked to Katherine, just a few days later, she told me that she had ended the relationship with her boyfriend. That night by candlelight, we both opened our souls and expressed how each of us truly felt about the other. It was really no surprise that we both had virtually same feelings for one another and on that night we "officially" fell in love. I remember driving to work that next day looking around and thinking to myself, "The whole world looks different."

For myself, finding my soul mate and life partner was very similar to finding God. It was something so *sure*, so *real* and so *right*, and an experience that was impossible to deny. Like God, I always believed she *existed* but to what degree I had no idea and after so many years of wondering and hoping and waiting my *belief* (like it was with God before I actually found Him) finally became a full-fledged *living reality*. And once again, as is so many times the case, patience paid off. It is absolutely true: "Good Things Come to Those Who Wait."

"Be in Love and You Will Be Happy"

Within no time Katherine and I were living together in my tiny house completely head over heels in love. We would have married each other after knowing each other just two weeks but figured we probably should wait. Besides there wasn't an ounce of fear or doubt in regards to how dedicated we were to each other. It was truly magical. And the energy between us was so powerful that if the two of us held a light bulb in our hands, it would have probably lit up. We spent every waking minute together (with the exception of work) but still it wasn't enough. In December, we started thinking that it might be a good idea to quit our jobs and take an extended vacation. That way we could be together 24-7. It sounded a bit eccentric especially to friends and family but, we knew that someday we would have the responsibilities that come with a home and children and work and that it would be decades before we would have this kind of opportunity again. With this in mind, we each gave our employers two weeks notice and began planning for a road trip that would eventually take us to the Florida Keys.

On January 1, 1991, we said goodbye to the little house I was renting and moved all of our belongings into the basement of my mother's home, the place I was so eager to leave only one year before. The past year had been pivotal for me with a lot personal growth and progress, but this would be a new chapter (more like a second re-birth) in my life and one that I couldn't wait to embark upon. No longer would I be going *solo*. I now had a partner/companion and finally felt *complete*. I was a little tough to put my drums in storage and my artistic dreams on hold but I couldn't wait to have the wife, kids and a house with a white picket fence. For these I would give up gladly give up everything.

After celebrating the holiday season with family and friends we packed up my future wife's 1990 Volkswagen Golf with camping gear and supplies and headed south with a return date of unknown. It was a fun and exciting trip and after a brief stay in Atlanta to visit with friends we arrived at my Uncle George's home in Coral Gables where we would spend the bulk of our time in Florida. We then headed further south down to the Keys where we found a perfect campsite right on the ocean. We would spend lazy, sun drenched days on the beach simply enjoying each other's company. I would read or strum an acoustic guitar while Katherine made beaded jewelry. For dinner we'd buy the local catch and grill it over a campfire. And at night we'd gaze at the stars and talk about the future. What a magical time!

In late February, after eight blissful weeks in Florida, we decided it was time to go back home and begin making the necessary arrangements for a spring wedding. Since money would be tight and not feeling the need for anything extravagant, we chose to get married on the grounds of her mother's home. It would be a small, intimate celebration with only the closest of family and friends present. My wife's sister Carolyn would be the maid of honor and her boyfriend and my good friend Scott would serve as my best man. Eight months earlier, Scott and Carolyn were introducing me to Katherine on the front porch of my little house. Funny the way life unfolds.

We were married on May 18th 1991 and it was the perfect day for an outdoor wedding. The air was crisp and refreshing due to a thunderstorm the night before that pushed some sticky, humid air out to sea. The sun was warm and the sky was deep blue. We couldn't have asked for a better wedding day and everyone had a great time.

For our honeymoon we took that entire summer off. We would spend most days at the beach lounging in the sun reading books or taking long walks. On weekends we would travel to Boston where we'd take in a museum or the many interesting shops (mostly used record stores) that were plentiful on Massachusetts Avenue. It had been a tremendous year filled with the happiness that comes from spending significant time with the person you love. But soon it would be time to get back to work and begin saving money for our future. In September my wife got a teaching job and I, in October, went back to delivering auto parts for the family owned business where all of this started.

The Soul Lives On

During that winter, with no change in my father's condition, my mother decided to have his feeding tubes removed. This was a choice that was not without controversy. My father's sister vehemently disapproved of such action thinking it just wasn't right because he was still technically "alive" but my mother felt that after sixteen months of life support coupled with seeing him in that state day after day after day, it was time to let him go and on December 23, 1991 my father passed away. As sad as this was for me I knew without a shadow of a doubt that he was *very much alive* and that we would see each other again and resume the relationship we once had but had yet to fully develop. For my mother (and my sister who had been by her side the whole way through) it had been a very, very long hard road and I was relieved to see that her long suffering was finally over.

In all the months my father was on life support I saw him only once. And on that occasion I had a complete and total emotional breakdown. To see him in that state was just too overwhelming and I remember thinking how wrong it was to keep him like this. At that point in my life I lacked the strength to endure the pain and sadness of seeing my father like this as well as the wisdom to understand the complexities and challenges that present themselves during times like these. But what I did *know*, even at that time, was that life is *everlasting* and that my father in the end would be alive and well and free with eternity straight in front of him. I am looking forward to seeing him again.

In February my twelve years of using marijuana both frequently and infrequently came to an end. This had been coming for quite some time since at this point in my life, I was only using once in a blue moon. After years of using, the effect it had on me started becoming an annoying distraction that *took away* from experiences as opposed to positively enhancing them. The electricity and excitement that it had once provided was replaced by a feeling of laziness and fatigue. And after becoming sober, I began to realize that great music is great simply because *it is* or that a hike in the woods is beautiful because it *is beautiful*. All these activities and occasions are fantastic in and of *themselves* and don't need anything artificial to make them better. It was refreshing to now experience life, all the time, on a completely real and honest level.

As time passed, the need for my wife and I to branch out and leave my mother's home was becoming more and more obvious. We had saved enough money for a small down payment on a house and began looking at real estate in our area. This was a sobering experience. Neither my wife nor I made a whole lot of money at our jobs and we soon discovered that homes in our immediate area were financially out of our reach. Instead of looking at homes in other parts of the state, we began throwing around the idea of building an in-law apartment onto my mother's house. This idea worked well for several reasons. One, the cost of an addition wouldn't suffocate my wife and I financially. Secondly, we could be there for my mother especially as she was entering her elder years and thirdly, it would allow us to stay in a part of the region that we both loved. We all agreed that this would work great for everyone involved so we began laying the groundwork for what would become a rather large addition. The plan was my mother would move into the new building and my wife and I would take over the original dwelling. Everyone's future was beginning to take shape.

Although this was an exciting and hopeful time in my life, the absence of pursuing my artistic aspirations was beginning to have an adverse affect my being. For years I had felt a strong need to live and to be true to myself as an artist and was now feeling a bit empty without it. So when the dream of owning a home became a reality, I made a promise to myself to resume that journey only this time I had a more clear picture of the artist I wanted to become: a *jazz* drummer.

During my time away from playing music, I had become a rabid jazz lover buying vintage albums at a record pace. My vinyl addiction took my wife and I all over New England and beyond in search of these rare and valuable treasures. I also purchased a set of 1960's Ludwig drums from an old jazz musician. These tubs were the "real deal." I spent a whole afternoon painstakingly removing old paint from the shells trying to restore them to their originally finish. I stored them in the corner of the basement knowing that it would only be a matter a few months before I would be taking them out, dusting them off and working them hard to fulfill that musical promise.

After my wife and I were approved for a 30-year mortgage, construction on our new addition began in the spring of 1994. Aside from some minor set backs and some major squabbles between my mother, my wife and myself, the building of this in-law apartment went smoothly. Little did any of us know that there was something very serious looming on the horizon.

The C Word

Beginning that summer, my mom developed a nasty cough/cold that none of us thought very much of. But as the weeks passed, her condition seemed to worsen to the point of having to see her doctor. To my wife, my mother's cough sounded eerily familiar for her father had died of lung cancer some ten years before. We all started to sense that something was seriously wrong given the fact that mother was a heavy smoker and had been for almost fifty years. Our instincts proved to be correct for that October, after an x-ray and tissue biopsy, she was diagnosed with lung cancer. I think that life is a lot of like the weather where you have a few days of relative calm followed by some disturbance that causes a change in the forecast. Sometimes the change is minor and sometimes it's catastrophic. If life is like the weather, this would be a category five hurricane.

My mother's cancer was a crisis that would catapult me into a practice that would continue to this very day: daily prayer. Trying to connect more firmly, more intimately with God was, once again, *essential* for me at this point in my life. Now more than ever, strength, courage, fortitude and resilience were needed (and received) in abundance. Not only for myself, but for all of us involved in this immense struggle. I would talk to God (pray) every morning on my way to work and every afternoon on my way home. At night I would meditate on God trying ever so hard to open my mind and allow His Indwelling Presence to comfort and sooth as well as strengthen and fortify my troubled soul. These practices would not only serve me well during the time of my mother's disease but they would be necessary for the challenges of the not so distant future.

Everyone who was close to my mother tried to be positive and optimistic about the fight that was about to take place, but it was my mom who seemed weak and unenthusiastic about the battle with cancer she was about to go through. She had already been though a lot so who could blame her. But still, the plan of attack would be to remove the lung that had the tumor within it. This would be followed by further treatment that would hopefully put her into remission and render her cancer free. When the doctors went in to remove her lung, they saw that the cancer had spread like wild fire and that there was little they could do for her at this point. When she left the hospital, she moved in with my sister who was better equipped logistically to take on the enormous task of caring for my dying mother. Once settled, she began to receive targeted radiation treatments in an effort to reduce the tumors that were sprouting up all over her body. There was nothing more painful than to watch my mother slowly wither away.

We had made plans to bring my mother to her home for the final weeks of her life, but she wouldn't last that long. On January 21, 1995 my mother died in her sleep. She was sixty-four years old.

The last couple of months of my mother's life were extremely painful both physically and emotionally for her as well as everyone who was closely connected to this struggle. It was heartbreaking to witness all the pain and suffering she had to endure but those last months gave us the opportunity to talk about many things. It gave me chance to express to her how sorry I was for all the grief I had caused her. I had been selfish and disrespectful as well as arrogant and insensitive for many years. I also got to thank her for all that she did for my wife and me. Allowing us to live in her home all those years virtually rent-free and eventually giving us her home was *enormous*. It also gave me time to, most importantly, say how much I loved and appreciated her.

It was and still is so very reassuring to *know* that when my parents died, we would be re-united in another realm and that the time apart would only be *temporary*. This is the one very real silver lining in what is so often times a very dark cloud. My hope is that they both knew that too.

White Pickett Fence

With my mothers passing, ownership of this now very large home, fell upon my Katherine and I. We finally had the home we had dreamed of but it would be minus the doting grandmother who would have adored her grandchildren. The feeling was bittersweet. But in the end, life must go on and it did. As a couple we began making plans for starting a family of our own. Individually, I began my quest to become a jazz drummer. I took my drums out of storage and began a practice schedule playing no less than thirty minutes a day. Each day I would work on different skills. My plan was to practice by myself (woodshedding) for one full year then I would attempt to play with other musicians. I stuck to this plan like glue.

That November, my wife and I conceived our first child. I recall feeling both fear and excitement in what we were about to embark on. But we were both as ready as we could have ever been. Most important was the fact that we were still madly in love. We now had the home, steady employment, and some money in the bank. And we had a sufficient amount of time alone together. All of our ducks were in a row. The time was right.

The birth on my daughter on July 21, 1996 was an epochal event in my life. Leaving the hospital I remember looking around me and thinking once again "everything looks different." And aside from the feeling of love I had for this helpless babe there was a feeling of enormous *responsibility*. The life of this precious child was in my/our hands! I knew I had to be a better person because parenthood would be the most important work that I would ever perform. But what was most comforting to know was that I wouldn't be alone in this endeavor. I had my wife and a solid marriage, good friends and family who lived locally and now more than ever the *ultimate parent* who resided within me: God.

Needless to say, the first few weeks of parenting required a great deal of adjusting. Newborn babies are completely helpless and need almost constant monitoring. But my wife (who would be a stay-at-home mom) and I were strong and unified and aside from some colic and sleep depravation, managed to settle into a comfortable groove.

Aside from being the trying to be the best father I could be, I was playing my instrument with a purpose and preparing for the next phase of my musical development: performing with other musicians. In January, I managed to connect with some jazz students who were going to the Berkeley School of Music in downtown Boston. Once a week I would pack my drums into my car and make the drive downtown. This is where I got my first taste of ensemble playing. It took awhile for the group to actually "groove" but once it happened, it was pure heaven. This was a fantastic experience but one that wouldn't last very long. The drive to Boston was tough enough but the effort it took to find parking on the street and then unload a set of drums, get them into the building and onto the elevator, up several stories then down a hall to a practice room, set them up, play for a couple of hours then do it all over again in reverse was crazy. It became way too much effort, which forced me into looking for musicians that were closer to home.

After trying out several players who didn't fit the musical idea I had in mind, I placed and an ad "Jazz Musicians Wanted" at a local music store. I soon received a phone call from two young horn players who were very serious about their music and eager to play. I'd had landed a bass player a few months earlier so with the addition of the two horn players, I had my first full fledged jazz quartet that rehearsed weekly in the living room of our large new addition. I got a great deal of satisfaction watching this group gel as a unit as well as the strides I was making personally as a drummer. My long time dream of becoming an artist was finally coming true.

On the home front, everyone was doing great. My wife was living her dream of being a mother and homemaker and our little girl, who was now almost two, was plump, healthy, happy and smart as a whip. Life was good but unbeknownst to my wife and I the most frightening day of our lives was just around the corner.

Crisis

The morning of July 8, 1998 began for me the same way as any other workday would. Up at seven-thirty, get dressed, eat breakfast, make the five-minute drive to work and punch in by eight o'clock. But this day would end in a much different way. About an hour after getting to work, a fellow employee approached me and said, "Your wife called and she needs you at home." When I inquired about the nature of this phone call he replied even louder and more emphatically, "Get your ass home NOW!!!" A wave of panic washed over my entire body as I ran to my car. The ride home was good in that it gave me a little time to gather my thoughts and tune into God's, now much needed, *calming influence*. I pulled into my driveway with a new mindset: feeling strong, fortified and ready for anything. I can't remember a time in my life when I felt so composed under such extreme duress.

What happened on that morning was when my wife went to wake up our daughter, she found that her body was limp and lifeless. She picked her up and held her trying to get some kind of response. When it became clear to her that something was seriously wrong, she immediately called 911. What my daughter had experienced was a mild seizure. I arrived home a few minutes after the ambulance and paramedics, who soon whisked her away to a nearby hospital. She quickly recovered from her seizure and after some tests we were all on our way home. When we got home, my wife and I cried our eyes out as our daughter talked and played as if nothing had happened. That night, I thanked God deeply for helping me get though what had been the worse day of my/our life. To get that kind of reinforcement the *moment* it was needed was simply amazing. This was clearly one those times when the spiritual rubber meets the human road.

There would be many instances in the years to come, hundreds perhaps thousands, where I would go to God for help and support and not once did God let me down. Not one single time. But that is just what you'd expect from someone who is totally dedicated and committed to *serving* you.

After my daughter's seizure, the doctors put her on a drug called Phenobarbital to prevent any further seizure activity. When a battery of tests and scans found nothing obviously wrong, we began to slowly wean her off of this medication. For a time it looked like her seizure would be a one-time phenomenon. Unfortunately, this wouldn't be the case.

As my family and I rang in the New Year and with my daughter's seizure seemingly behind us, my wife and I started planning to have another child. We were all at a great point in our lives yet I found myself going through a different kind of crisis: a spiritual one. Not with my own relationship with God but with what I *wasn't* doing as far a helping other people spiritually. If you had the cure for cancer, or in this case, the cure for the broken soul, how long could you keep it to yourself?

Everyday I would talk at length with people who were broken or maybe even slightly cracked; people that were in need of love, support, wisdom and guidance; people in need of friendship and companionship, all the things that God gives to all of us *in spades*. Or I would talk with folks who were sad and lonely, or struggling with addiction, or perhaps they had just lost and loved one. The list goes on and on and I would always walk away for those conversations wishing I could do more for them. And I found myself thinking more and more, "If they only knew God what a *difference* it would make." I would turn on the nightly news only to learn about the latest mass shooting or another case of domestic violence, of murder, of rape or of child abuse. Not to mention all the greed, fraud, waste, abuse, corruption and thievery that happens every second of every day. The list seemed endless. I'd look at history (past and present) with all its conflicts and the death and destruction they produced, the terror and oppression, genocide and ethnic cleaning, sectarian violence and on and on and on. It was just plain horrifying and the more I learned about these tragedies, the more driven I became to do something about it. But I wanted to do more than pray (still, an important act of love and form of effective service) for people or just hope that they would be O.K. I wanted to help people find the *remedy* for themselves and tap into this *original source* of all things *good* and reap the many *immense* benefits that God provides *first-hand*. The only questions were when, where and how?

In June, my wife (who was now five months pregnant) my daughter and myself took a trip to California to attend the high school graduation of a young woman my wife used to baby-sit for. During our visit, my daughter suffered a second seizure. Although she recovered from that event, a dark cloud of worry and uncertainly hung over us for the rest of our time in California. When we got back to New England, my daughter was put back on daily medication and was soon diagnosed with epilepsy. My wife and I had a feeling that this would be a very long and challenging road for many years to come.

The Turning Point

Going back to when I first found God I had dreamt of ways of sharing my discovery with others. The problem had always been that I lacked the wisdom and knowledge that comes from experience needed to accurately put into *words* (spoken or written) the experience of knowing and working with God. But by the late nineties, after going though so much in my own personal life and knowing God they way I did, I felt I had finally acquired enough wisdom and life experience necessary to become a teacher of spiritual truth. One of the things I discovered over the years was that while most people believed in a God or some "higher power", what they did with that belief was put it in a small box and place it in the way back of their mind only to bring it to the forefront of their thinking once in awhile, mostly in crisis situations. It was hardly the immense, full-blown, *everyday working partnership* that it could be. For fifteen years I had known God intimately and applied His wisdom and loving influence, literally thousands of times, to my marriage, my job, raising a child, dealing with my family and on and on and through all of it reaped *immense fruit.* And although I felt like I was ready and had the *ability* to start teaching people, I still had no idea as to *how* to go about actually doing it and *where* I would be doing it. More importantly could I muster up courage to do this work without training, without formal religious education relying solely on my living experiences both with and without God and finally, could I muster up the courage and audacity to proclaim to people, "These truths I *know!*"

How did I know? In thinking about *what* I would actually be teaching people, I knew I didn't just want to simply repeat or regurgitate what someone else had told me or something I had read somewhere. Now that's *not in any way* me trying to de-value or diminish the importance of speech and text, teachers and books. I am writing this book and you are reading it and a person can gain a great deal of knowledge and wisdom from textbook/classroom-based learning but at some point, you have to get outside and get your hands dirty. You must get out and live life and *engage* the world. Or in other words, become street-wise. I would formulate teachings that would be based on my life (the good, the bad and the ugly) and my spiritual experiences (working with God intimately). Besides, this was all I knew. And with this knowledge, my objective as teacher would be (and will always be) to guide a person *beyond* the realm of academic study all the way to the *real living experience* of God who just happens to be a *real living being*. Nothing can say as much about God than knowing and working with Him on a personal, intimate level. This is the *final say* spiritually speaking. And how someday you too will *know* what is true spirituality.

On October 20, 1999 my wife gave birth to a healthy baby girl we named Olivia Ann Smith. And although our oldest was now three years old and becoming more independent, with our new arrival we felt like we starting all over again, which of course we were. But there was almost immediate tension between my wife and I caused by lacked of sleep as well as being on constant alert and all the other stresses that newborn babies create and I felt right away that this would have to be our last child. I expressed this to my wife who was understandably less than pleased with my ultimatum. I personally had a very hard time with the newborn and infant stages of parenting. So much so that I found myself looking forward to Mondays so I could get back to work and away from the laborious task of catering to an infant child. I knew I didn't possess the patience and stamina it would have taken to go though this a third time and was not about to "push the envelope." And though money was certainly an issue, this was more about a "wise person realizing his/her limitations" which was/is crucial in trying to live a *balanced* and *healthy* life. In the end, I truly believed that having another child would have been the straw that broke the camel's back both emotionally and financially.

Within a couple of months my wife and I (seemingly) settled into a peaceful groove and with the new millennium approaching, life was looking pretty good. As we got closer to the New Year I found myself chomping at the bit to get started with my new endeavor of working with people spiritually. As I was searching for ways to reach people, I happened to drive by a hand painted and very amateurish looking sign that simply read, "Advice by Perry." Now mind you, this "Perry" on the sign was an actual certified psychiatrist but it gave me an idea: make yourself available to people who are seeking *spiritual* advice. I thought about making up business cards with my contact information on them. From there people could meet with me somewhere or we could talk via the telephone. A friend of mine also suggested using a personal computer and the "web" for their live online chat rooms and message boards as another viable way to reach people who might be hungry spiritually. I began thinking if I could do something with people along the lines of what my friend did with me (conversation) the night I found God, it should be effective in helping the people I'd be working with find God and therefore *experience Him*. I immediately got online and began to look for religious chat rooms for the purpose of gaining practical experience in discussing God with others. These online chat rooms would become the ideal venue for me because it gave me access to a whole world of different people with different ideas and also, and more importantly, I wouldn't have to leave the house. This was something I could do at midnight when the whole house was asleep. The one thing I was adamant about was not letting my new passion interfere with my family life.

My work as a teacher of spiritual truth began on January 1, 2000. My hope was that the new millennium would naturally raise the over all level of human awareness and people would be hungry for a new kind of "spiritual awakening." My deepest dream was to revolutionize the way people think about and approach God and to usher in a golden age of spiritual enlightenment that was *finally* rooted in True Spirituality (knowing and working with God on a personal, intimate level) the likes of which has yet to be seen on our planet. One that promotes a gradual shift from doctrine study and rote exercise to a real, active, personal, dynamic living relationship with the Supreme Creator Himself. (Spiritual truth mind you, whether it is in God or in love, in peace or in wisdom, in family or in friends is a *living experience* first and foremost) My avenue for accomplishing this "awakening" would be by formulating teachings based primarily on the similarities between the God experience and the positive human relationship experience drawing on the parallels between the two: One, because the *same principles apply* and secondly, it is a truth that most human beings can *relate to*.

Life at home was becoming increasingly stressful and tense as my wife and I seemed to constantly be at odds. I had the relatively easy job of driving around by myself delivering auto supplies while she labored hard at home with our two young children. Like most mothers she was over-worked, under-paid and under appreciated. She even took on the additional task of watching our niece and nephew. When you add this to breast-feeding a baby, sleep deprivation, overall self neglect, an older child (who suffered another seizure on Feb 14) with epilepsy and a husband who could have been a lot more attentive and you have all the ingredients for real clinical depression.

That spring, tensions between my wife and I came to a head when after a night at work (I was now working two nights a week to supplement our income) I came home to find both my wife and our youngest daughter in tears. My attempt to intervene lead to an argument that resulted in my losing my composure and calling my wife probably the worst four letter word a man could call a woman. With that one word I had instantly tore her heart out as well as my own and she came within an inch of asking me to leave our home. Our relationship was at an all-time low and it would be quite sometime until we would be whole again.

As I was spending most of my free time trying to help people spiritually, unbeknownst to me, my wife was slowly descending into the abyss of depression. The seriousness of real depression was foreign to me. I knew my wife was down but not to the extent that she actually was. My thinking was that it would soon pass and she would be back to her normal happy self but her pain was too deep and now becoming all consuming. It can make you feel helpless at times because you realize that while your co-operation and support is essential, you can't go inside a person's mind and find peace, happiness and satisfaction for them. In spite of all these challenges my primary goals were to simply be there for her, help out around the house as much possible and lastly, to never lose my composure again. It would be a time when, once again, working with God on a daily and sometimes hourly basis would critical in getting me though these extremely difficult times.

The Chat Room Years (My Education)

One of the few bright spots for me during these rather hard and difficult times was getting my feet wet talking about God in online chat rooms. My initial experience online was finding rooms that were anti-God or anti-religion where I would try to convince people of God's existence while they would try to convince me of God's non-existence. My bold effort was an abject failure for one very good and timeless reason: the people in these rooms weren't *seeking God*. It was a strong lesson for me in regards to *who* I should be sharing this truth with. I mean, if the stone cold fact of one's own *existence* itself hasn't convinced them; if this vast *planet*, teeming with *life*, that we all reside on hasn't convinced them; if they can look up at the night sky with its million of stars and not think that there is a God/Creator, then tell me *what words* could I possibly *say* to a person that would suddenly bring them to the realization that there truly is a God? Without God, there would be *nothingness* and you cannot open your eyes anywhere without seeing *something* (proof).

Without a *creator*, there would be no *creation*. But still, if that person was just as *immoveable* in his/her feelings about God as I was, no one was going to budge. And it started becoming not only a waste of time but also an exercise in *futility* plus annoying to those people that simply weren't interested in hearing about God. In the end, it did help me learn one very valuable lesson: sharing spiritual truth is like giving someone advice: you give it when *asked for it.*

I was started to gain confidence and a little bit of momentum in these chat rooms when a summer lighting strike knocked out many of our household appliances, one of them being our personal computer. As hard as it was to be isolated from my new passion (obsession) it did allow me time to think about what I had learned online. And it was around this time when I started to put to *paper* some of the topics that were discussed in these online rooms. Not being a writer I found the task of putting what I knew in my mind into the written word challenging but nonetheless, it was something I felt driven to do in hopes of someday being published and in turn reaching *more people.*

The more I thought and wrote about these truths, the more I realized that the God experience moves in very much the same way the positive human relationship does, especially the bond the exists between a parent and his/her child. With God, you're working with someone who is constantly *perfect* and perfectly *constant*: someone who is tireless and never unavailable, someone who is *all knowing* and someone who working from the *inside out*. We humans on the other hand are imperfect, inconsistent, limited by time and distance and can only work from the outside in but *make no mistake*, good people are *just as important* to have in one's life as God is. I would also come to think of religion and spirituality as a sort of dartboard where you have this enormous amount of space that is filled with the many different beliefs and theories, myths and superstitions, ideas and philosophies, books and other sacred texts and so on. Some are further away from the center and some are closer to it. But at the *very center*, you have the *bull's eye*, which on this dartboard represents God and more specifically, God's Living Presence Within You. I would forevermore base my teachings and now my writings around these very basic but central truths with the goal being to help the reader hit the bull's eye i.e. *find God*.

In a few months my family had a new computer and with it my lines of communication with the online chat world were once again wide open. But this time rather than being a visitor in other people's rooms, I would create and host my own chat room where I could provide spiritual food for the spiritually malnourished as well as basic foundational support for those people who were in need of some. My hope was that this would become a serious, consistent, reliable, *open* venue for anyone who curious about God or anyone looking to share and express his/her own knowledge and experiences spiritually. I decided to title my room "Finding God" with the hope of attracting more sincere seekers and because that's what my purpose in this room would be. My goal was to help the individual understand who, what, when, where, why and how God is and *ultimately* how to find God for themselves. I came to view this room like a dating site where I would be the "matchmaker" bringing two, God and the individual, together as one. I would come to see myself as a *conduit* that someone forgets about once the *connection* with

God is made. It then becomes their relationship to develop over time. I would accomplish this by using the same *formula* that had helped me some sixteen years earlier at that tiny gas station: person-to-person conversation. And I would model my *method* of helping people find/experience God on what worked for me that very first night I found Him: being alone in a room with God.

My new chat room as you might imagine was quite compelling and would generate interest from atheists to religious zealots, from the mildly curious to people who were just looking to agitate. Many of the teachings in part three of this book were gleaned from the back and forth conversations that took place in this online chat room. Here are some of the more frequently asked questions and topics discussed . . .

1. What does the God experience mean? I will give it size and meaning as well as depth and dimension in this way: think about the most important relationships you have in your life: your best friends, your spouse, your parents, your grandparents, your children and so on. Now think about how much they

mean to you and the role they play in your everyday life. If you took just one of them away, you are left with a hole inside of you the size of a crater. The God experience is a *living relationship* of that *magnitude*. It is more than just casual association it's a *gigantic* one on par with the deepest most significant relationships in your life. And furthermore, to *experience God* is opening yourself to His influence (love and wisdom) and allowing that influence to have a positive affect on you.

2. Why does God allow bad things to happen? Probably the most frequently asked question, God's *supreme wisdom* is total and complete. He created humankind to possess a dual nature: positive and *negative*. He also endowed humankind with another attribute: Freewill. When you combine these truths, there is the *potential* for bad things to happen. Sure we would all love at times for God to overtly intervene in the affairs of humanity. Do the dirty work for us. But this is obviously not how God operates. It is up to us as to how we manage this world and the life that God has so

lovingly given us. Yes indeed, bad things do happen because of our *nature* coupled with the fact that God *allows us to be free* (if you love someone, set them free) but they do not *have to* happen. Bad things are sometimes the price of freewill but I ask you, "Would you rather not be *free*?"

3. What is the meaning and purpose of life? I call it the three G's, Goodness, Growth and Giving. To be your best self, to progress and develop and to share with and serve others. Purpose: to better yourself from *within* and they way you see and treat *other people*. Imagine what our world would look like if its occupants truly lived life's meaning and purpose.

4. What is the foundation of life? The foundation of life is wisdom, love, guidance and support *in the form of* positive, living, intimate, long-term relationships both in people and (if you so choose) in God. It is a *living foundation*. Not only are these relationships vital in promoting the true meaning and purpose of life (compelling you to move in a positive direction as well as providing internal emotional fortification)

they are *central* to over-all, long-term, personal *happiness* and they teach and inspire us. And by their *example*, they show us how to become moral and ethical and they make doing the "right thing" easier. Without a sound, solid foundation, a structure will start to lean and if it's not reinforced it will eventually crumble. This truth is also directly related to the question of why bad things happen. More often than not it is the *lack* of true love and sound guidance in the form of a solid, living support network/ foundation.

5. What about things like Hell and Armageddon? With God, places and events such as those are *simply not possible*. God is *too* good, *too* perfect, *too* loving to create such a place or commission such an act. I realize words like "incapable" and "impossible" seem odd when describing the attributes or the actions of an all-powerful Creator but when it comes to plagues, baby killing, eternal torture, worldwide destruction and favoritism those words are entirely *valid* and completely *accurate*. In short, God's Perfection (not my opinion) renders these

things *impossible*. Always, always, always keep in mind that God is *Perfection Absolute*. Anything less simply is not God.

6. What about the role of the devil and possession? I just don't see how it would be possible for some outside force to penetrate the human mind that houses the Living Presence of God. It would be like trying to put your fist through the hull of a battleship. We grow up and live in a world where the power and difference between good and evil seems negligible and perhaps in this less-than-perfect world, it is. But as we move forward towards goodness, growth and giving the potential for evil becomes less and less until it becomes totally *non-existent*. As it is with God.

7. Why does God judge and punish us? Besides knowing "how many hairs are on your head", God knows your every thought, every intention, every incident, every act, every detail, every fiber of your entire being and your entire history (from the *inside*) not to use against or judge you but to have *total understanding* of not only who and what you are but *how you got there*. God knows

where you stood yesterday and where you stand today. His concern is your present direction and where you'll be tomorrow. As far as punishment is concerned, the fact of the matter is God doesn't punish us for the simple reason that God doesn't have to. Human beings are endowed with the ability to feel emotion, to experience guilt, shame, embarrassment, disgrace, humiliation and so on. We reap the *consequences* of our freewill thoughts, actions and behavior. What goes around comes around; we reap what we sow and we more often than not, we get our just desserts. So you see, God doesn't have to punish us because in essence, *we punish ourselves.* Ask anyone who lives with guilt. That's not to say that simply feeling bad about a serious crime should be enough of a punishment in the eyes of society or that more serious crimes don't warrant a more severe sentence. It means that wrong doing itself and the guilt that follows can torment (punish) a person for a very long time. It's human and justified to want to see wrongdoing judged and punished. It's spiritual to want to see wrongdoing rehabilitated and wiped clean.

8. What about the connection between drugs and spirituality? It's very similar to steroids in sports where some might promote their validity and effectiveness it's tough to feel completely comfortable about their use and to endorse them. And although I have had experience with drugs, I never used them as an avenue for enlightenment. The problem with drugs is that they can be extremely dangerous to one's physical and mental health and their effect is temporary. God's Loving Influence doesn't wear off in a few hours it becomes stronger as it is exercised and is anything but bad for you. If you take a look at the 1960's, the people certainly had the right ideas in peace, love and brotherhood but because these truths weren't constructed on a solid *spiritual* foundation, the movement eventually crumbled. God provides the firmest and most *lasting* footing you will ever find. And besides, how can you have a Brotherhood of Man without the Fatherhood of God?

9. September 11, 2001 was day that brought
    a lot of visitors to my chat room asking
    questions and looking for answers, I was
    too. This relates directly to God allowing
    bad things to happen. God could easily give
    a tyrannical dictator a fatal heart attack five
    years before the genocide begins or the mass
    murderer an aneurysm twenty-four hours
    before the shooting spree begins or steer the
    deadly hurricane out to sea. God leaves the
    affairs of this world entirely in our hands
    while *at the same time* He is actively working
    within each and every one of us *individually*
    to help us to *better* ourselves from within
    (progress) and the way we see and treat
    other people (love).

10. What about Forgiveness? Forgiveness is
    something that we human beings struggle
    with. It seems to be in our nature to hold
    on to grudges and not to forget them. We
    desire to see bad things happen to bad
    people and going back to the consequences
    of our actions that is, more often than not,
    precisely what happens to bad people. To
    God, we are all rare, precious and beautiful
    and God never grapples with forgiveness in

the same way we humans do. With God, like so many His qualities, to forgive is *automatic*. Once again, God is *incapable* of anything less. But God, being Perfection Supreme, takes it a step further in not only helping us to forgive each other but also in helping us to forgive *ourselves*.

11. What about the fear of God? Fear and intimidation in God served an important purpose in bringing about order and obedience to the brutal and savage world of the past. It kept people on their toes morally and ethically which lead to great advancements in the societal behavior. The problem with fear is that it can become overwhelming and all consuming and become a real hindrance in regards to *greater spiritual enlightenment* if it is not curtailed. Always keep in mind that our Creator, once again, is perfect in everyway and you should never feel intimidated or fearful when looking into or thinking about this Perfect Parent who created you. The last thing a good parent wants is for their child to be afraid of them.

12. How is God served? Throughout history much blood and much treasure has been given to God in the name of sacrifice and service. But God seeks a different kind of treasure, the greatest of all treasure: love. True Love moves in a circular motion. When someone is loved, they are compelled to give love to others, which goes back to God. Love is another word for service; service is another word for love. To unselfishly serve your fellow human being is ultimately how *you* serve God and how *God is served*.

The time I spent ministering to people in this chat room were some of the most gratifying in my life. It was in this room where I would come to know and understand the value and meaning of true *service*. And it brought out in me truths I never realized I knew until I was asked the questions and had to really think about the answers. When I could work one on one with a person (via instant messaging) and they were open minded and seeking, it was magic for both of us but towards the end of my tenure in this room, it was becoming more and more frustrating and contentious.

After a time, my chat room became less about assisting the seeker and more often than not, a place for people who were simply looking to lock horns and debate religion or toss around spiritual concepts, which is *great* but that wasn't the reason I was there or why I was created this room. It was never really about showing off one's theological knowledge or how many people you could get to agree with you. Much to my chagrin I was spending most of my time there simply defending my relationship with God as opposed to enlightening the curious. Some would question my credentials pointing out the fact that I wasn't educated religiously or sanctioned by an organized authority therefore who the heck was I to teach people about God. Some would ask, how can you or anyone really *know* these things about God? (No person can look inside another person's mind and tell them what they know or don't know) Others seemed to be threatened by what I saying which I could understand *if* what I was teaching wasn't positive and true. (If you are absolute in your spirituality, nothing or no one should sway you in the same way someone who is secure in his/her relationship need not worry about the attractive neighbor) To the religionist I was a fool who couldn't possibly know God because I didn't read the proper text (Is what something someone, who I've never met or talked to, wrote in a book suppose to trump *my own living relationship* with God?) or follow the right religious figurehead. To the non-believer I was a fool to even think that God existed in the first place. I soon found myself hovering in a sort of "no man's land" which was/is a very lonely place inhabit.

In the end, I came to realize a couple of key truths: It's not a matter of who's right or who's wrong or who's intelligent or who's ignorant or who's well-versed in written text or who isn't, it's about *who you know.* Also, after spending so much time talking to so many people, it dawned on me one day that there are ultimately two kinds of people *spiritually speaking*: people who know God and people who do not. Anyone can read, memorize and recite reams of religious literature but true spirituality will always, once again, boil down to this one basic truth: a person either *knows* God or they do not.

In addition to the frustration I was experiencing during my time online, many of the people in my rather large circle of friends and family knew of my spiritual work yet hardly anyone would inquire as to what it was about or what I was trying to accomplish. I found it amazing (and still do) that something so *immense* could mean so *little* to so *many* people. Perhaps people with strong human support feel not the need for spiritual support. And lets face it, there are some not so wonderful people and events associated with God and religion that can naturally turn people off and away from God. But always, always keep in mind that these negative aspects of spirituality come from the negative aspects of *human* nature and should not and *cannot change* or *diminish* the actual greatness of God for He is *absolute* in His *perfection*. Yet still, a lot of the time, just the mere mention of God could generate ambivalence in a person. Overtime I found myself using the more benign term "spiritual" in place of God simply because "spiritual" is a word that most people wont run away from.

It is true that we don't have to find God in the same way we don't have to look for that special someone, or have children or develop deeper friendships. These relationships *are optional*. I know plenty of people who aren't interested in (some for good reasons I am sure) these associations and they seem to get along just fine. But when we open ourselves to these *cornerstone relationships*, the rewards are *tremendous* and in my estimation, *vital*.

Hard Times

By the fall of 2001, I had enough written text to create a website. My hope was that the site would go viral with people going there by the thousands to view this amazing work. This never took place. But still I kept plugging away in my chat room trying ever so hard to teach and influence people spiritually. I could see I was growing as a teacher and was feeling really good about where this work was heading but on the home front, things couldn't have been any worse.

Both my wife and I were beginning to buckle under the pressures of life with young children and all of the stresses that go with it. We began keeping score of how much "free time" each of us had and if the number seemed imbalanced, the other would become indignant. I would lie about my whereabouts to go record shopping or I would get home late from work because I took the long way home on my motorcycle. Eventually she would find out about these indiscretions, which caused her to lose trust in me. This was devastating to our relationship. She would express to me over and over about how she didn't need me and how she could do all this *by herself.* During this time I living on a steady diet of criticism and felt like I couldn't do anything right. There were many times that I thought to myself she must have married the wrong person and it wouldn't have been surprised if one day she came up to me and said, "I've had it, and it's over." Fortunately, that day never came.

While it's certainly true that these were painful and trying times, I never wanted to throw in the towel on our marriage and call it quits. I knew deep down that there was a real and special bond between us that would outlast any of the hardships that we were facing at this time. My feeling was that if we remained a unit and worked together would we eventually get through this and eventually we did.

At my job, things weren't a whole lot better for me. There was real and measurable level of animosity directed squarely in my direction mainly because I represented two things most people find detestable: wealth and privilege. Wealth because of the rather large and valuable home I lived in with a very small mortgage, and privilege because I was the boss's brother-in-law. In their eyes I was a slacker who was unwilling to take on more for the company. And looking at it objectively, I could understand their feelings. Delivering was easy and I was the boss's friend and brother-in-law. I was neither comfortable being a salesman nor was I really qualified to be one, which showed in my performance or lack thereof. I would decline offers to work *inside* the store, which drove some employees crazy. I just couldn't get excited about an industry had no real passion for. I never wanted a *career* in auto supply, (trust me, a solid auto parts counterman has to know a million things. It is hard work and a serious profession) I just wanted a job. A job I didn't have to think about after five o'clock and a job that easy with little stress. This way, I could focus on my true passions: music and spirituality. But rather than buckle under the pressure and quit a job I *liked* for a person I *loved*, I'd try to become the best driver the business had ever seen.

Although I would never become an authentic auto parts specialist, I was a reliable, dependable, accurate delivery driver that developed into a somewhat serviceable sales rep. I always tried to have a positive attitude and was pleasant to employees and customers alike. If anyone had a problem with me I would simply "kill 'em with kindness" and by-and-large this worked well for me. Ownership, who couldn't have been better with all of this, recognized my strengths and simply let me be to do my job. But nonetheless the tension I felt there was real and each day was a challenge. My goals there, like at home, would be simple: be strong, always stay composed, be kind and respectful and always strive to "take the high road."

I do not mean to or wish to come across as "whoa is me" or "I was right and everyone else was wrong" with all of these struggles both at home and at work. There were no good guys and bad guys here. Most of the time it was simply differing points of view, which is good and healthy. Still we are all, at some point in life, challenged by something or someone and the challenges I faced at this particular time were very real and very significant. And the reasons I write about them are not to *indict* anyone but to *illustrate* how important it is to have a solid support system and especially the role God played in getting me through these rather difficult times.

Thank God

After spending so much energy on my marriage and the challenges that presented themselves at work, patience with my children was in short supply and I was hardly the good father I should have been. As much as I tried, I could never seem to keep my composure when it came to dealing with childhood issues. But *once again*, my daily practice of morning and evening prayer coupled with almost continuous conscious spiritual awareness (I was basically clinging to God daily) was essential for me in coping with both my work and home life. These habits were critical in two ways: one, they helped me get through the day in one piece by providing immediate "in the moment" strengthening and secondly, they influenced my overall *long-term* growth and development as a human being.

There is no question in my mind that these most significant relationships in my life would have likely fallen to pieces had I not been spiritually fortified. Never would I have made it through without the *internal* support from God and the *external* support from the people closest to me. And I am certainly not the person I am without either of them.

With all that was going on with my marriage, my children and the people at work, my online chat room and making music with my band were two of the few places that I actually felt good about myself. Positive, productive conversations in my chat room would energize my evenings and have my walking on air the entire next day and I soon found myself becoming addicted to the satisfaction that comes as a result of helping a fellow person. I actually didn't mind missing weekly band practice (which was unheard of) because it gave me the opportunity to open my chat room where I might meet someone who was interested in knowing about God. Once I got a taste of real *service* and the happiness and fulfillment it garnered, it became all I wanted to do. It was a really magical time for me and hopefully for the people I was talking with.

Getting Better

My wife began receiving personal counseling for her depression in the spring of 2002. It took a great deal of courage and determination to face her dilemma head on and I admire her greatly for that. She realized that she would stand a better chance at recovery if she had some professional, objective outside help and she was right. We all witnessed an immediate change in her personality, attitude, outlook and overall state of being. With each passing month she grew stronger and more confident as well as becoming simply a more happy and peaceful person. It was an amazing transformation that just goes to show how important it is to have self-respect and personal integrity *within* in addition to positive, living support *without* for all of the challenges that this life presents to all of us. It's also critical for the long-term goal and purpose that is "to better one's self from within."

When my website failed to yield the results I hoped it would, I found myself back at the drawing board. As great as it is, the computer screen can seem rather cold when you compare it to something that you can touch and hold in your hand. This time, my vehicle for helping would be in print on paper. I began working on what would become a pamphlet (and eventually this book) while delivering auto supplies at work. Whenever a pertinent thought came to mind I would quickly jot it down. Most of what I was writing down was based on the previous night's chat room conversations. Using my website as a starting point I began to construct what I hoped would be an epic piece of spiritual literature that would change the way people think about and approach God. I would dream about people in homes all across the United States as well as the rest of world making this epic discovery. A discovery that would change their lives and lives of the people around them until everyone knew what the experience of knowing God was all about.

Beginning in December of 2003, I began the painstaking process of gathering up and trying to put into order the dozens of little notes scribbled down on scrap pieces of paper. I would spend the next four months trying to separate the wheat from the chaff and turn my pile of written rubble into a cohesive composition that I would title after my website, "Finding and Knowing God." The primary challenge would be (as it always is and especially if one's not a writer) to put into the "written word" something that is a *living experience*. Writing in this way was like trying to describe the sound of music or the flavor of food. Words fall way short. But regardless of these obstacles, I labored hard over each sentence making sure it was the absolute best I could make it. I was quite happy and proud of this achievement and besides my chat room this written work would provide me with another tool to help people find God.

Mid-Life

When I completed my little booklet in March of '04, I decided to take some time off from spiritual work. It was also around this time (a few months away from my 39th birthday) that I began going though a mid-life crisis of sorts. I was finding that I didn't have the same energy and stamina I once had; my eyesight was getting progressively worse; I had developed gum disease; I was beginning to notice lines and wrinkles on my face; my pants were feeling tighter around my waist; aches and sprains that once went away in a few days would linger for weeks and months; my sex drive was noticeably down which naturally caused my anxiety level to go up. All of these worries came to a climax when I found myself in the emergency room of an area hospital.

I was at the grocery store on a gorgeous summer Saturday when I began experiencing these funny heart palpitations. I first experienced these same symptoms the previous August after ingesting some energy supplements to help get me though working nights. Only this time, I wasn't taking anything. As the hours passed I could feel myself growing more and more worried, which intensified the heaviness I was now feeling in my chest. At this point I became sweaty and my breathing was erratic and I thought for sure I was experiencing real, serious heart trouble. In my mind I was going though all of my recent mid-life concerns that only intensified what was now a full-fledged panic attack. I made an excuse to get out of the house and drove myself to the ER where I was given a few tests and a drug for anxiety. After reading the results of scan, the doctor explained to me that my heart was occasionally skipping a beat, which caused the next beat to be stronger, and this is what

I was feeling in my chest. He also suggested that I see a cardiologist if I felt his explanation wasn't to my liking. By now, the medication they had given was working and I was feeling relaxed and a little embarrassed. I drove myself home feeling relieved but also a bit concerned.

Two days later I woke up with the same heart palpitations and once again the panic machinations were set in motion. My wife and I wasted no time in going to a different hospital that specialized in cardiology. Once again I found myself in an ER with a doctor who told me pretty much the same things the previous doctor had. But knowing this wouldn't be enough for my now fragile psyche, he scheduled me for a stress test and echocardiogram. This way I would know for sure that I didn't have a life threatening heart condition. The problem now was that the tests wouldn't be for another month!

I woke up the next morning feeling down, depressed and completely shell-shocked. How could I, Mr. God-knowing, emotional, psychological titan be reduced to a sack of rubble in an emergency room chair? In a matter of a few short days I became week and frail. All I wanted to do was turn off the lights, close the shades and go to sleep. But deep down, I knew that would be the worst thing I could do. I talked to God (prayed) long and hard that morning to be *fully receptive* to His encouragement and supreme influence. I needed now more than ever the extra strength and confidence to get up, get moving and get my mind and spirit back to where it had once been. Sure enough, as always, God would not let me down. The first thing I did was to mow the lawn.

The following month, waiting to take my cardio tests, would be a day-to-day struggle emotionally. I still wasn't wholly convinced that my heart palpitations were completely benign. Every time I would experience any kind chest discomfort or felt the slightest bit dizzy or light headed I would feel the wheels of the anxiety machine start to turn. I would have to do everything in my power to keep that small spark from turning into a raging fire and for the most part I was able to do just that: keep it at bay. Even to this day I still feel susceptible to anxiety's unjustified yet debilitating grip.

After an excruciating month, I went back to the hospital to take the cardio tests that I hoped would confirm my physical well-being and give me the psychological assurance my mind so desperately needed. After completely all the tests and consulting with the cardiologist I was given a clean bill of health. After hearing those few magic words I could feel the stress I had been harboring for many weeks *instantly evaporate.*

The entire experience gave me a shot in arm perspective wise and I began to live life with a heightened sense of purpose and determination. I realized that my time here on this earth is finite and I should no longer put off my goals and aspirations, especially my dream of helping people spiritually.

That fall, my first order of business (besides getting life insurance) was to produce copies of my booklet for distribution. My goal was to go to small area bookstores to see if they would be interested in selling these small booklets. I even sent a copy to the program director at Boston's National Public Radio station with hopes of doing a live program about God. I turned my defunct website into a place where people could order my booklet. Everything was now in place for me to begin my next phase of trying to help people find God and with that, change the world.

Six months later, after so much hope, I found myself feeling the same way I did two years earlier, down and dejected. My booklet never made it into any bookstores because I lacked the drive as well as the confidence needed to approach people about

my work. I never got on the radio either. But I did manage to get these booklets into a few people's hands. I did this primarily through my online chat room where I would mail copies to people who were interested in reading it. I gave some to people I knew personally. All in all I gave away about fifty copies to mixed reviews. For some, it lacked the fire and brimstone, shock and awe, the volume and power and the pomp and circumstance that many people envision when they think about God. Some liked it for its simplicity and straightforward message. But for most people, at twelve pages, it simply lacked depth. It just wasn't meaty enough. And with that I would have to agree but it was all I had. Once again, I would be back at the drawing board but this time, I would be out of ideas.

When things didn't go quite the way I hoped they would with my booklet, I began to question my abilities as a teacher, a writer and the whole notion of trying to change the world spiritually. My online chat room was all but dead. About one out of every twelve people who came into my chat room (that is if anyone visited my room) were actually interested in knowing about God. The other eleven were people, like I stated earlier, were folks who were either looking to debate the reality of God which after my initial lessons online I had no interest in doing or they wanted to discuss religion and theology, which I knew next to nothing about. I had always been there to assist the seeker but at this point there just didn't seem to be many people looking.

When none of my many spiritual endeavors reached the height I thought they would, I found myself on the verge of another mid-life crisis only this time, it wouldn't be health related. This crisis had everything to do with what kind of work I would be doing for the rest of my life. Being a delivery boy was really great in many respects. It was a low stress, low impact job that gave me ample time for thinking and introspection. I could stay in touch with news and world events via radio programs on the many news stations. I had the freedom to do small errands or get a bite to eat. I also did most of my spiritual writing while driving. But more than anything, it got me out to where I met many great people who I would develop meaningful relationships with where I could put my now more mature spirituality (a true and real love of people) in *motion*. But at the end of the day, it still wasn't the work that I was most passionate about. I knew I had more to offer than delivering automotive parts and fast food, the question was *what*. I began considering something I never dreamed I would do again: going back to school.

The thought of returning to school was indeed a scary one but also an exciting one. First and foremost, I had the *massive* responsibility of supporting my family who needed shelter, food, clothing, heat, transportation, healthcare and everything else that goes along with it. Where would I find the time? Secondly, I had never really been the academic type. I always preferred learning something via the experience of doing it and on my own terms. And lastly, what would I go to school for? After the work I had done helping people spiritually and after experiencing how gratifying it could be I decided that I wanted to help people but on a personal, intimate level. Perhaps counsel people in a way that was similar to what I had been doing with folks online. Psychology seemed to be the obvious choice and besides, I had taken a psych class in community college and was fascinated by it getting an A with hardly any effort. With this in mind, I paid a visit to a local college and spoke at length with one of the guidance counselors about what I wanted to become and what it would take to get there.

I left the school feeling really enthusiastic and at the same time overwhelmed. The amount of time and effort it would take to re-invent myself and get my degree would be significant. And it would certainly take away from the already limited time I got to spend with my wife and two daughters. After spending the next few months weighing all these factors, I decided rather than taking the time, energy and financial resources it would require to earn a degree in psychology, I would re-dedicate myself to my true passion: helping people understand, find and experience God.

If ten times you don't succeed, try again

With the idea of going back to school firmly in my rear view mirror, I re-directed my energies on new ways of getting my teachings out into the mainstream. My first order of business would be to re-write and re-title my booklet, which I was never completely satisfied with. And after some serious thought, I discovered I had a lot more truths to express, truths that could be injected into a new composition.

That fall of 2005 I had my new booklet and with it set out to distribute them in area shops that seemed appropriate for the kind of work I intended to do spiritually. This time however I would paper clip a business card to my booklets that contained my contact information. This way people who wanted more information could contact me for live, personal support. I also found myself returning to my online chat room. The same room I opened almost five years before. I had come full circle.

On January 9th, 2006, I placed a phone call to an independent publishing company to ask about getting my most recent booklet published. While the gentleman on the line explained to me that this was certainly possible, he suggested what I might want to do is expand on what I had already written and turn my small composition into an *actual book*. While that thought had crossed my mind in the past but I never really took it that seriously for the one simple reason that I am not a writer. My twelve-page (now nineteen page) booklet was a real struggle for me that took years to get right so just the thought of writing a "real" book was a daunting one. But for all its shortcomings, the booklet was a noble idea and one that was worth rewriting and polishing into a book.

With an actual book, I could give people a much more meat and potatoes, in-depth, inside look at what a working relationship with God is like, what it can provide and how it relates to the "Human Experience" (based on my twenty-three years of knowing God) as well as answering *every* question that *anyone* might have about God and true spirituality. I could not only raise the bar regarding the *definition* of God and clarify the many misconceptions *about* God but also up the ante in regards to *personal* spiritual enlightenment and the discovery *of* God. It could also be an alternative pathway for people who had given up on traditional religious teachings and serve as a beacon of truth for the hungry seeker in his/her quest to understand, find and know God. And with a subject that is *universal* (*everyone* thinks about God at some point and to some degree and most people wonder about where they came from and where they're going) and a subject who is *perfect*, *permanent* and *absolute* and with an audience that consists of *all people*, how could I go wrong? Furthermore, with me working so much and time being at a premium (any kind of serious discussion about God should take between two to three hours if not more) I found myself having less time to devote to people in need. One of the great things about a book is that the author can be in a million different places *at the same time*. So in essence, where this book goes, I go. Where this book is, I am.

I began working on this book shortly after my phone call with the publishing company. The following would be the guiding principles for this book as well as my life: Always be respectful and open minded when it comes to people's religious beliefs and spiritual pathways; be honest and accurate about yourself, your life and what you know about God Himself; write and speak straight from your soul; always keep the spotlight of spirituality pointed squarely on God where it should be with the spiritual *end game* being to help the reader to find and experience God on a personal level. Now all I needed was a title.

After considering new titles such as "Sixty Seconds With God" "The New, New Testament" "Box of Light" "Where's God?" and "What's Been Missing" (with a period and not a question mark) and "Find Me!" (Where I would write as if was God writing the book but after some serious consideration thought better of it), I finally settled on the title of my most recent composition: "The God Experience." First because nothing says as much about something or in this case, *someone* than one's own experience with them and secondly, it's essentially a book about God: the mountain top of spirituality; the bulls-eye on the spiritual dartboard; the most high, most perfect one, none above, all below, all-mighty creator and *love supreme*. To combine the two you to have, "The God Experience."

I have felt shaken at times and certainly defeated by all these spiritual failures, but never completely broken down. And there have been times over the years when I considered giving up on trying to help people spiritually. But every time I thought about calling it quits, something would happen (as inevitably happens to all of us) in my life that would challenge me. And as always, I would lean on God for internal support, guidance and fortification and *without fail*, God would always come through for me and I would think, "There's no way I can give up on this work." This truth about God is simply too important for me to keep hidden away within myself. In fact, I think I'll open my chat room right now. Maybe the person on the other side of my computer screen will be you.

Afterword

It is 8:28 Sunday morning April 2, 2006 and my wife and two children just left for church. You might be wondering why I am not with them. For me, the entire world is my church and everyone on this world is my congregation. Besides, prayer and worship has always been something that I prefer to do in private. At this point in my life, things are going well. My marriage is better than ever and my wife has made great strides with her depression. She works very hard home schooling our kids, keeping our home in order and bettering herself from within. My daughters (now six and nine) are healthy and steadily growing, with my oldest being seizure free for over five years now. They will always be my highest priority and I love them both more than anyone in this world. I still struggle to keep my composure with them mostly when they are just being kids. It really isn't very fair for me to get angry with them just for acting silly but I am working on it. I still find time to play jazz with the same group of guys from '97 and we even get paid for it once in a great while. When I am not delivering fast food or automotive supplies or spending time with my family, I like to spend time buying records, listening to music, reading, watching sports on T.V., motorcycling, fishing with friends and of course working with people spiritually which is ultimately why I wrote this book. So through all the ups and downs, hardships and struggles I will continue to live, work, grow and give to others.

Revision 2012

My book was published in 2006 and although I was proud of my accomplishment I still found myself reticent to share this news with *everyone*. Deep down, I knew it just wasn't *complete*. Still, I gave many copies away and sold a handful. I sent a bunch of books to reviewers from around the country hoping some of them would find it valuable and endorse it. Looking back, the book was good, not great. I wrote the first two parts, my life story, in three weeks. Part three, "Teachings", was basically the same text that made up my nineteen-page booklet. I simply joined the two parts together. It was sparse, incomplete and certainly rushed and at ninety-two pages, wasn't exactly "War and Peace" but its intent was, as it still is today, to prevent war and promote peace. Still it was not the epic, earth shaking, world changing piece of written work that I hoped it would be which is prompted me in February of 2012 to revise and essentially re-write the first edition of this book in an effort to give it the weight, width and depth that it so desperately needed and that the first edition so sorely lacked. Its goal now is the same as it ever was: to serve as the bridge or catalyst that takes you the reader all the way to the experience of God Himself. If it can do that, then it has served its purpose and I have done my job as a teacher. I hope you will be one of those people.

Ever since the day I found God I have been dreaming of ways to share that discovery with others. It's been a rather long road in trying to make this dream a reality. It started with a business card fourteen years ago, and then there was a pamphlet followed by a web page. An online chat room became a book. When the book wasn't a success I tried an online radio program. When that flopped, I created a children's book that never really got off the ground. As you have read so for, my spiritual work has been a series of attempts and failures.

My life however, has not been and I attribute that to having such a solid living support foundation both within *and* without me. It is this truth that keeps me coming back to the dream of changing the world via "true spirituality." Regardless of the course this new book takes, I will always try in some capacity to help those who *want* to know about God for it has become such a part of me. It is now in my blood forever. And I will do this work not for fame, fortune, glory or recognition but because spiritual truth, and love being at the center of it all, is simply too important, too meaningful not to be shared.

Afterword 2013

It is November 24, 2013 and I just got home from church *with* my wife and two children. I started attending church about two and a half years ago for the purpose of *family unity*. I still prefer to pray and worship privately simply because I can connect in a greater way with God when we are alone together in the same way that my wife and I can when it's just the two of us. And I need not a mediator or go-between spiritually for I work *directly with God*. That's not to say that group prayer and group worship doesn't work for people. It obviously does and has for millions of folks all over this world. Church does many great things for many people and I would have to be blind not to see that. I see it most every Sunday. It can provide immediate goods and services as well as emotional support for those in need of them and is chock full of good people who are outwardly passionate about and inwardly conscious of God, which I find refreshing in today's world. But most importantly, it provides love and support in the form of positive living relationships, which is and will always be the most important truth in the universe.

My marriage to Katherine is even stronger than it was seven and a half years ago when I composed the first Afterward for this book and it will be stronger seven and a half years from now than it is today. That's what true love does: it grows. My wife works hard everyday educating our children, keeping them safe, maintaining our home and bettering her Soul from within and the way she sees and treats other people. She is also the most moral and unselfish (even to her own detriment at times) person I have ever known. The woman truly has a heart of gold. My daughters, now seventeen and fourteen, have been become wonderful young adults. My hope is that someday they will find partners who are equally as wonderful. They will always be my highest priority and I love them both immensely. I still find time to play music with, believe it or not, the same core group of guys from '97 every once in awhile. Everyone is so darn busy. When I am not delivering fast food or automotive supplies or spending time with my family, I still like to spend time listening to music, watching movies, reading, following Boston sports, motorcycling, hiking, biking, and spending quality time with friends and family and when I get the now rare opportunity, working with people spiritually. Perhaps with this new book, those opportunities to work with people wont be so rare. I am looking forward to what the future has in store for me. No doubt it will be challenging (it's suppose to be) but with all the love and support I have in my life both within and without, I am sure it will be positive, productive and ultimately, gratifying.

TEACHINGS

The truths contained in these teachings were derived from several sources and have grown over the years as I have. They are not based on years of extensive theological research. They are not based on speculation, theory or conjecture. They are not based on what I think or feel God is or what I hope and dream God is but what I *know God to be*. They are ultimately the by-product of my twenty-nine years of knowing and working with Our Father on a very personal, intimate level. But I would be remiss if I did not give credit to the vast living support foundation I have had throughout my entire life starting with two great, loving parents who provided me with a wonderful childhood. There is also my partner Katherine who shares with me a strong marriage, an amazing friendship and two beautiful daughters. And not to mention the many friends and family who have loved me over years and who I love very much. But most importantly, many of the deep truths I know about God come from being the *father* and parent of children *myself.*

Many of these truths also came as a direct result of answering questions in my online chat room. And a great deal more from my forty-eight years on the playing field of life: the struggles and challenges, the successes and failures, the victories and triumphs. But there is another source and one that I cannot emphasize enough and that is free and independent *thinking* coupled with the desire to discover and know. Thinking is like traveling: it's supposed to take you to a destination or *realization.*

The purpose of these teachings is not to convince, cajole or convert you. They are not meant to be provocative or controversial. They weren't created to compete with, put down or criticize other forms of religious and spiritual inspiration. I did not compose them to challenge age-old, time-tested established beliefs. And I didn't write just so I could flex my own spiritual muscles. I did not write them to preach to people or lecture to people or tell people how they should live and what they should and should not do. I wrote them to inform and enlighten, lift and illuminate, to educate and inspire and ultimately *assist* you the reader in finding and experiencing the love, peace, wisdom and perfection of God for *yourself* with the broad-based goal of helping to change the *entire world*.

Although they may come as a surprise to some people, in most cases I am simply stating the obvious: that God is perfection, that love is the answer, that goodness is the way forward, that the human race is one family, that spiritual truth is a living experience and something that you become, that life is what you make it, that true wealth is measured in the amount of good people in one's life and that there is ultimately great meaning (love) and great purpose (progress) to this life.

Introduction (Why God)

You are a *freewill creature*. You do not have to open yourself to anyone and allow them into your life. You don't have to expose your thoughts and feelings, beliefs and opinions, worries and concerns to anyone. You don't have to ask anyone for help or assistance. You can certainly "Go it alone" and in a sense we all do. But your life can turn on a dime and when you stop and think about all of the unpredictable, hazardous, crazy things that this life, this world and other people can thrust upon you, partnership and companionship; the power of *we* and the power of *us* and the power of *two* is something all of us should seriously consider.

Individual pride, strength and independence are important, valuable attributes worth possessing and exercising, so to is humbling yourself to allow others to love and assist you. It is not a sign of weakness to ask for help, it is *wise* and often times necessary due to all the challenges we face as human beings. There are the challenges that come with youth and inexperience; with going to school and a career; with sex and sexuality. There are the struggles that come with marriage and raising children; the challenges that come with growing older; of sicknesses and diseases; of death and dying. All of these challenges are important aspects of life that teach us about strength and courage, growth and wisdom, service and sacrifice. They compel us to rise, grow and progress or stay the same or worse, regress. But with all these hardships there is an equalizer. There is something that can tip the scales and help a person get through *any* of life's many pitfalls as well as the personal faults and shortcomings all people possess: a *foundation* that is made up of positive, living, intimate, long-term *relationships*. And if a living support foundation is something that you lack, finding God is a very good place to start building one with.

To have someone with you to celebrate your victories and comfort you in defeated; someone to teach and inspire you; someone who challenges, motivates and brings out the best in you; someone who provides you with company and companionship; someone who cares about you; someone who will love and hold you *unconditionally*; someone who makes you feel safe and protected; someone who encourages you to grow and give of yourself to others; someone who is a true friend and loyal confidant who will stand by you through thick and thin. These are the absolute truths that positive relationships can provide and the very reasons why it is worth finding and getting to know God.

At the end of the day life is ultimately about these living relationships: mothers and fathers, brothers and sisters, aunts and uncles, grandmothers and grandfathers, husbands and wives, best friends and family and on and on and on. Not to diminish the value of casual encounters or part-time acquaintances but these are the *bedrock relationships* that make up the pillars of a solid living support foundation, the foundation that we should all build our life upon. This is how *true wealth* is measured and makes crystal clear the meaning and purpose of life. Those who have an abundance of living support are truly the richest people in the world. It is God's *desire* to be part of your foundation and play an active role in your life. The purpose of these teachings is to not only encourage and promote these cornerstone relationships but to help you add this other layer to your already existing foundation: a *spiritual* one. And the more layers you add to your foundation, the stronger it will become.

There are many different forms of inspiration that can help a person find God just like there is many a service that can help a person find their significant other. Some avenues, if they are living, might become a close friend. Some you may never see again. Others, if they are material, might rest on a bookshelf or become a favorite place to visit.

These pathways will always occupy a special place within us but let's not confuse the path with the destination. The spiritual pathway can also be memorable and exciting but what's most important, and it's true with any avenue, is getting to the *final destination* which is, spiritually speaking, God's Living Presence Within You.

We live in the "Information Age" and there are many ways to garner religious and spiritual teachings. And with all the different pathways to enlightenment at your fingertips you are bound to find one that works personally for you. It might be the religions of Judaism, Buddhism, Hinduism, Islam or Christianity. It could be the text in the Bible or the Koran or the Talmud or perhaps the teachings of Jesus, Moses, Abraham, Isaiah or Muhammad. For some people it might be art and music or movies and television. For others it could be poetry and literature, philosophy and religion, someone in their own family or the next-door neighbor or perhaps even a stranger. Some people have outside help and some people find God completely on their own.

Different avenues work for different people and as long as it is not *harmful* to someone's mental and physical well being I say, "Great!" Different venues work for different people as well. For me it was a dark room by myself, for others it could be a small place of worship and for someone else it might be a mega-church with twenty thousand parishioners. Whatever becomes your catalyst always remember this: your relationship with God will be *incomplete* until you open yourself to God's Presence and allow His Perfect Spirit to enter your *conscious mind*. There are many spokes on the spiritual wheel of inspiration yet only one *hub*. There are many corridors in this mansion but only one room where God resides. Ultimately, we all must go to the same place to truly reach God and that place is *within*.

When looking into the God here are a few things to keep in mind: all roads spiritually should ultimately lead to God; aim high when your climbing this spiritual mountain and take it all the way to the summit; ride the metal rails of the Spiritual Dartboard towards the bulls-eye and not away from it and take this spiritual journey all the way to the *finish line*. And as you pour over the miles of written text and hear the spoken words of many a teacher, do so with an open mind; do your best to separate the wheat from the chaff, never throw the baby away with the bathwater; always keep your "Spirit of Truth" radar *on* and your common sense and instinct antennae raised *high*. And when you ponder God or if someone makes a statement regarding God ask yourself this question, "Is that perfection?" Furthermore, you should never feel afraid, intimidated or threatened in your quest to find and know God. This is *Good News*! God is good, positive, bright, uplifting, liberating, and by-all-means *Free*. Anything less simply doesn't apply to Him. God is everything God *should be*: real, permanent, perfect, present, dynamic and *active*.

Tools and Abilities

You, reader, are an amazing being. In addition to your unique, one-of-a-kind, no one else in the entire universe *personality*, you are endowed with incredible tools and astonishing abilities. You have the ability to recognize what is true and what is false; to know the difference between what is right and what is wrong; between what is love and what is hate; between what is civil and what is savage. You can learn the difference between what is good and what is evil, between arrogance and humility and between what is sour and what is sweet. And not only do you possess God; you possess the tools and abilities to *find Him*. All you have to do is put them to use.

Your body is a temple capable of grace and beauty, strength and recovery. You have eyes to *see* and ears to *listen*. You have a voice to *express* yourself. You have hands to *touch* and hold, a nose to *capture* fragrance and a tongue to *taste* many different flavors. But most importantly, you have a mind to *think*. A mind that can solve problems, gain knowledge and grow wiser; a mind that can dream and imagine, contemplate and wonder, question and deny, to doubt and be skeptical but also to be open to discovery and realization. Not to mention a mind capable of common sense reasoning; a mind capable of being logical and sensible, instinctive and intuitive, creative and spontaneous. And it is within the *mind*, with help from the *Spirit* that shapes and constructs the human *soul*. You also hold a heart to *feel* the entire spectrum of feelings and emotions. You can experience love, joy and bliss, happiness and delight as well as anger and hatred, envy and jealousy, sadness, remorse and regret. And with all these tools at your disposal, you also have the ability to *exercise them*.

Of all the abilities human beings possess none are more significant than the abilities to exercise *choice* and *decision* via *freewill* and also to *experience first-hand* the wonders of life, discovery and of human nature itself. Let's take a look at the duality of human nature, that tug-of-war within pulling you one-way and then the other. God has *designed us* in this fashion and insists that we experience *both* the positive and negative aspects of our nature for a very good reason and purpose. Why? Should we love or hate? Should we help or hurt? Do we build or destroy? Do we enslave or set free? Now these questions become a *choice* for you see, without the experience of *both* there would be no true understanding *of them* and therefore understanding of the differences *between them*. What would be the point of choice and freewill if there was nothing to choose from? The ugly and the negative not only provide us with *contrast* but they *enhance* what is beautiful and positive. And without the negative there would be no folly, no sin and no shortcoming and therefore no *challenge*. The negative is there for us to experience, look square in the face and eventually, through choice, hard work and with help from others, put *behind* us. The negative is not only there for us to learn and grow from but also to *transcend beyond*.

Without these qualities and attributes we would all be ready perfect like a machine. But it would be a machine that *didn't earn* its perfection. It would be a machine without a soul, without a heart, without a mind and without a challenge; a machine incapable of learning the profound lessons that come by mistakes made (wisdom) and never to experience the joy and satisfaction that comes from personal growth and loving service. It is all of these things that make life so compelling, worthwhile and *gratifying*. Especially when a real *step forward* is taken and progress is made.

Living Experience is your greatest teacher and God knows this, which is why God has endowed you with this most invaluable ability. Living experience and academic study both have merit and value. There's nothing wrong with spoken and written forms of truth. I am doing that here on these pages right now and your doing it by reading them. But take skydiving for example. You can read about it in a book or have someone who has done it describe it to you. Or you can get in that plane, strap on that parachute, climb to ten thousand feet, take that leap, freefall for a mile then pull the ripcord. Now the question becomes, *what means more*? What means more, reading the menu or eating the meal? Reading the sheet music or hearing the song? Having someone describe to you what true friendship means or having a true friend? Watching something on T.V. or actually doing it? With these examples in mind I ask you, "Don't you want more?" It's the *same with God*. Trust me, nothing says as much about God than to experience God on a personal, intimate level.

They say that a picture is worth and thousand words. If that is true then the experience is worth a ten million.

So you see, there is a great reason why you possess all these qualities and abilities: So that you the *individual* may find, feel, discover, realize, recognize, learn and grow for *yourself* and of your own *freewill*.

Indeed "all people are created equal" in Body (Tools and Abilities) and in Spirit (God's Living Presence) but it is personal *choice*, will, desire, drive and determination that set us apart. Environment and upbringing is not a life sentence. You don't have to wallow in your shortcomings forever. You can be anything you want to be. You possess the tools, equipment, and abilities to not only exercise Spiritual Truth but also to find, experience and "become it." Whatever or whoever it is that you long to find be it truth, happiness (true success), knowledge, wisdom or a better life; be it friendship, your soul mate; God or even yourself; if you work hard, play fair and keep your nose clean; if you pay attention to what's within and around us; if you are respectful of others; if you are thoughtful, aware, open minded and receptive; if you are diligent and persistent, you *will find* whoever and whatever it is that you seek.

Spiritual Truth (5-5-90)

Spiritual Truth (truth that directly relates to God) is not only something that I live and something that I teach, it is also who I am and what I am. But still, I do not own it. It is not my sole property. It is also not my invention or my creation: it is God's. It belongs to everyone in the same way God belongs to everyone. Spiritual Truth is love, peace, wisdom and balance. It is integrity, pride and self-respect. It is patience and humility. It is calm and composure. It is discipline, moderation and restraint. It is strength, courage, fortitude, endurance and resilience. It is freedom and choice. It is growth, betterment and progress. Spiritual Truth is something that you give to others in love, respect, compassion and tolerance; in empathy and understanding; in kindness, courtesy and generosity; in loyalty and trust; in dignity and equality. It *cannot* be bent, twisted or destroyed and it is not subjective. It is permanent, eternal, constant, timeless and *absolute* and like the human soul that embraces Spiritual Truth, it is *indestructible*.

Spiritual Truth can be broken down into what I call 5-5-90. It is 5% written, 5% spoken and 90% *living experience*. It is 90% something you live, exercise, practice and demonstrate and over time it is something that you eventually *become*. Spiritual Truth without this *living component* can become just whole bunch of facts and figures and technical data. But still, laws and rules, guidelines and regulations are essential for governments and institutions. They are also vital for young people who lack life experience as well as older folks who may be for whatever reason, morally bankrupt or emotionally, intellectually and spiritually immature (childish). But in the same way experience goes beyond words, the becoming of Spiritual Truth goes beyond the mechanics of duty and good behavior and beyond the practicing of law-abiding codes of conduct, obedience, compliance and obligation. It can *start there*, but the more you live this truth, the more you expand the *positive* within you to the point where the it is so pervasive that negative within you becomes completely *expelled*. It reaches the point where virtues, morals, ethics and values become *automatic*. The internal struggle between right and wrong no longer exists because to do what is right becomes who and what *you are*, like it is with God. You *become* "the right thing"; you *become* "The Golden Rule." Even if you've never been *around* positive truth, that doesn't you render incapable of *becoming* spiritual truth.

There is reason why that when we are exposed to something that is true, it strikes a chord and resonates within us. Why it "rings true" and what makes it "self-evident." It's called the "Spirit of truth" or the spirit of *cognitive realization*. It is when the light bulb over your head is illuminated. It is a gift that all human beings are endowed with. But God not only gives you the ability to recognize truth, He is constantly and tirelessly working within you to *become* truth and to *give* truth to others which is woven into the fabric that is the meaning and purpose of life. And the greatest of all truth being *love* in the form of positive, *living relationships*. Love is the driving force that propels these truths into *action*. To know and live these truths will truly "set you free."

God's Nature, Presence, Will and Perfection

The depth, scope and complexities of God's Mind as well as the depth and magnitude of His far-flung, infinite universe of time, space, matter, gravity, planets, solar systems, black holes, etc. are truly mind-boggling and astounding. Just thinking about God in this way can be overwhelming and somewhat intimidating. There is not a word in any language that can describe just how deep and immense God *actually is*. The universe and all it's mysteries are indeed incredible and awe-inspiring and certainly there are many aspects about God that are beyond our understanding: we are simply too young. But when it comes to the *nature* of God, it really isn't complex or mysterious at all.

In describing and defining God's nature, two words immediately come to mind: Simple Goodness. A smile to a stranger, a compliment, holding the door for the person behind you, a reassuring pat on the back, returning found money, stopping for a stranded motorist, letting someone out in traffic, a random act of kindness, donations, charity and volunteerism and on and on and on. These are *tangible acts* of goodness even the most primitive person in the world can grasp the meaning of. They are the simple good works and deeds that we all witness all around us, most everyday. These acts may seem small and trivial but they are deep, timeless, significant and true. When you witness or experience the smallest or largest acts of service, kindness, courtesy, caring and compassion you get a first-hand glimpse into the nature and essence of God Himself. And let us not forget about God's greatest attribute: Love.

Love is a small word that means *everything*. It makes the sunshine and the world turn. It holds the universe together. Without love there would be nothingness and with love, eternity. I see it everyday. People want to be loved and should be. Everyone has something to say and everyone wants to be heard and paid attention to. Most people will welcome someone who takes a genuine and sincere interest in them. I have talked in depth with all kinds of people, hundreds of people from rough and tumble bikers to young receptionists and everyone in between. Whether they were young or old, rich or poor, black or white, *everyone responds to love*. I wish I could be a close friend to all people for I love them that much but, for obvious reasons, I *cannot*. Our Father in Heaven on the other hand, *absolutely can*.

I bet if you really examined all the ills in this world that had to do with human emotion, behavior and relations, you could trace most of them back to a lack of true love. Call it sappy or sentimental, if what is wrong with this world is the question, then love *is the answer*. Love may not be "all you need" but it is the foundation upon which everything; your life, the world, the universe is *built upon*. Blood may run thicker than water but true love always runs thicker than blood.

God's love is a love that is pristine, flawless and undiluted; it is infinite, boundless, constant and eternal. It is deeper than the ocean and as wide as the open sky. God's is a love that is powerful yet gentle; a love that can make you cry a thousand tears of joy and lift you to the highest of heights. God's love, like God Himself, is pure and perfect in every way, shape and form. God is love of the highest order that requires no sacrifice, no conditions and is given in abundance with *no strings attached*. God's love will make you *feel* warm and blissful yet at the same time, it compels you to roll up your sleeves and get to *work*. And it is God's Living Presence within you that, among many other things, can channel this love directly to you heart *every single time* that you open your mind to Him. God's love is a love that's all encompassing and long, long over-due in this world.

It has been said, "the Lord your God is with you" and it is *true* but our Supreme Creator has taken this truth a step further by sending His Holy Presence to *dwell within us*. God may be an unfathomable distance and dimension *away* from us here on this earth but by giving us each His "Holy Spirit" to live within us, God couldn't possibly be any *closer*. It is by this technique that God, via His Perfect Spirit, serves and ministers to us, imperfect, physical human beings. "The Kingdom of God is Within You" *indeed*. But it is *not* a Kingdom that is made up of dirt and sand, brick and mortar. It is a *spirit gift* and the *true miracle* that *everybody* possesses and has *access to*. Everyone on this world has a direct line to God in the form of this Presence. It is not something you have to ask for or travel to some far away place to acquire. If you're human, you qualify. It matters not how you came into this life. It matters not if you are young and old, rich and poor, man or woman. You *are*, therefore *you have God*. The Holy Spirit is there because *you exist*. And He is there to be a loyal and true friend, a loving parent and devoted soul mate (literally) all in one whose love, wisdom, knowledge and understanding are *totally complete*. He is there to be a teacher and guidance counselor whose commitment to you is constant and unshakable 24-7-365 *eternally* in order to help you form a more perfect *you* and to form more perfect *union* with God.

Everything God is and everything God does is perfect and flawless. God's love, wisdom, influence, devotion and *method of service* to His children, is perfect. Every single fiber of this immense and incredible being is without fault. God is constantly perfect and perfectly constant. And it is within this Divine Perfection that lay to rest any such notions about God being hateful or jealous, angry, wrathful or vengeful, bias or discriminatory. God's perfection *instantly negates* any such attributes rendering them *impossible*. Let us not *ever* make the mistake of giving God *our*

Father who is perfect in every way, shape and form, *human* faults, shortcomings and imperfections.

"Be perfect, therefore, as your heavenly Father is perfect" is a tall order indeed. There are a lot of faults and shortcomings for we humans to overcome within us as well as the many challenges we face from without us. But when you stop and think about what we as human beings possess: all of the innate tools and abilities, a mind fortified by God's divine Presence within (God truly did "Create Man in His *own* image") and a solid living support system without, the seemingly *impossible* becomes increasingly *probable*. God wills the human soul to become perfect because *it can be*. And who better to work with one's soul than the One who *created it*. Not only does God help you to see that all people are your family (brothers and sisters), but beyond to think of others as if they were your *own children*. This kind of *advanced spirituality* is a sure sign that you are not only becoming God like (divine) but also that you are truly doing the *will of God*.

It may be difficult for us to fathom perfection because we human beings are so far away from it. There are a million rungs on the ladder to perfection but God gives us *eternity* to reach the top. Perfection is not only who and what God is: it is our individual and collective *destiny*.

The Human Soul and God's Influence

The human body is temporary housing for what lies beneath the surface: The Human Soul. There truly is so much more to a person than meets the eye. Soul, like love, like God, may be a very small word but it means so very, very much. Who you are and what you are; your true essence; all the qualities that are uniquely and unmistakably *you* are housed in this invisible vessel. Impervious to sickness and disease, your soul is one-of-a-kind. It is the only one in existence. It cannot be cloned, duplicated or manufactured. It holds your personality, your character and your attitude, which are manifested in your words, actions and behavior. It contains your knowledge and experiences and with that your wisdom. It contains your dreams and ambitions; how you see the world and how you treat your fellow soul. It's what truly defines you the *individual*. The soul is what holds the contents of your *entire being*. It is ultimately the soul of a person that we fall in love with and who we become friends with. And it is all these aspects of your soul that God is working to *advance* (working with your conscious and sub-conscious mind) via His Perfect Living Presence.

When your life here on earth has expired and flesh and blood become dirt and dust, it is your soul that will *live on*. It has been said many times, "You can't take it with you" regarding one's material wealth upon dying and it is true but your soul and everything it has become, is the one thing, the only thing from this life that *you can* and will take with you into the next realm. When the time comes for you to depart *this world*, it is your soul that will be resurrected *on high* in a new body to continue its journey towards perfection and God.

Life, at its core, is really all about soul. Its present state, its growth and development and the kind of support it has around it. We as human beings are naturally drawn to place each other (and ourselves) into boxes and compartments and give each other titles, tags and labels but what truly matters most is the kind of soul a person possesses and the *direction* in which it is taking. This is what matters most in life and certainly what matters most to God.

The human soul can go in three different directions: forward, neutral or reverse. And I will illustrate these directions in this way: Neutral looks like two parallel lines six inches apart. If look down the road a mile, they are still *six inches apart*, in two miles there are still six inches apart and so on. When you take those same two lines and bend them toward each other you have reverse. If those lines continue in that direction, they will eventually become a point. And finally, if you take those same parallel two lines and bend them away from each other say five degrees, you have forward. If you look a mile down that road, those two lines are nine hundred and twenty five feet apart, at two miles they are eighteen hundred and fifty feet apart and so on. The soul that is moving in this (forward) direction will ultimately reach the shores of perfection, where it will finally "see the face of God." A neutral soul is simply spinning its wheels without movement saying in the same place. Reverse direction, if it is not changed, eventually becomes a dead end and with it, soul extinction.

This is the danger in wrongdoing: it can become habitual to the point of no return. Soul death (the ultimate consequence of living life in a reverse direction) occurs when every last drop of light within that person's soul is extinguished. Only the soul that is totally empty, *completely exhausted* of its potential for goodness will cease to exist.

Although it is invisible to the human eye the soul is revealed (manifested) though one's words, actions, deeds and behavior. It can certainly be judged (not in the final sense of course), but not destroyed by others for it is not made up of blood and tissue. Only its owner, via a wicked mind, can do that. The soul is eternal and indestructible when it's moving in a forward/positive direction and susceptible to extinction when moving in the opposite direction but *make no mistake*; even the most severely damaged soul (and one that has not changed direction during its earthy sojourn) if it has even the *smallest speck* of light, *will retain God's Presence* and upon *physical* death *will be* resurrected on high and given the opportunity to *change course* and *begin anew*.

God does not keep one child safe from harm while another child dies in some freak accident or from some deadly disease. God *is not* a puppeteer. God doesn't create a beautiful day for one family while another family perishes from a natural disaster. Or provide one family with a great bounty of food while another family starves. God *is not* "Mother Nature." God does not control people or manipulate the physical material world and the natural phenomenon it produces. God sphere of influence is confined, not surprisingly, to the *human mind* for to aid and assist it in the development of the *human soul.* So much of what we struggle with as individuals is *internal* which is exactly why God has positioned Himself there within where His love, wisdom and guidance can be most *effective* and once again, where it *matters most.* If you want to change *what's* within you, why not work with *who's* within you.

God's influence is like sunlight. True worship is pulling back the shades within and allowing His light to permeate and infiltrate your conscious *thinking* and with this have an affect on your *actions* and *behavior* as well as your overall personal *development.* A mind that is open to this perfect influence (love and wisdom) will experience a greater degree of overall peace, joy, happiness and contentment over a mind that is not. God's influence will not only improve one's overall *mental* health but it can also, by reducing stress and unnecessary worry, play a significant role in one's overall *physical* health and well-being and with this, the ability *to prevent* sickness and disease. "A Cheerful Heart *is* Good Medicine" indeed.

One of God's greatest attributes is *restraint*. God is indeed all-powerful, all knowing and all-everything and could obviously have his hands into every aspect of a person's life as well as the affairs of this entire world but He *resists*. Our Father, with all His *infinite wisdom*, does not. Why? Because not only would this kind of control negate freewill, but also because when something is *earned* via an honest *effort*, it yields the greatest amount of joy and satisfaction as well as *wisdom* for that individual who has done the hard work to get there. Doesn't the person who climbed the mountain with their own feet and hands and the sweat off their brow experience a greater sense of *accomplishment* than the individual who took the five-minute helicopter ride to the summit? God could of course do all the work for us in the same way a parent could do his/her child's homework for them but, would that be the best way for the child to learn his/her lesson? God is there to *help* us do our homework, not to do it for us.

Knowing and Working With God

"You shall love the Lord your God with all your heart, with all your soul, with all your strength, and with all your mind . . .

How can you have personal peace with a troubled mind? How can you have world peace without brotherhood? How can you give love to others when you don't feel loved yourself? How can you care about others if you feel that no one cares about you? How can you do well unto others if you feel that no one is doing well unto you? How you become *like* God if you don't *know* God? How can you be or become anything *by yourself*? God is your *personal* sponsor and champion for your growth, forward progress, soul development and happiness all the while being a loving parent and close friend.

God is actively working within you, for you, *right now*. This is what a living relationship means and what knowing and working with God is all about: from the *inside* out.

When you open yourself to someone and allow then into your life; when you spend time together, work together, communicate with one another (prayer) and connect with each other (worship) not only will you get to know them greater but you will also bear the fruits of what that someone is *giving to you*. And not only that, your *relationship grows*. Spending quality time with and good friend, someone you love, invigorates and energizes you and if he/she is wise you will garner a great deal of wisdom from them. The more time you spend with that someone, the more their influence starts to rub off on you. When you tap into God, or any positive influence for that matter, you are likely to become better simply from being *around them*. If you're around water enough, chances are your going to get wet.

Any relationship must be *maintained* in order for it to be a meaningful one. It takes time, commitment, dedication, effort and *consistency*.

These are all the same truths that God practices with us so in order for us to reap the benefits of knowing God, *we* have to practice them as well. This relationship is most definitely a two-way street. You have to work *with* God. Your openness and participation are paramount in order for God's influence to be *effective*. You have to be *receptive* and the more open you are, the easier it becomes for God to assist you. And as you *work* together over time, this relationship will become a real, bona fide *marriage*: an impenetrable bond and unbreakable union.

Lets get one thing straight, finding God is *not* an instant magical miracle cure-all concoction. Finding God does *not* make you or the world around you perfect overnight. It doesn't make problems and challenges, old and new, magically vanish into thin air. Profound change *takes time*. Your growth, development and in some cases *recovery*, is and should be a *gradual process* that requires patience as well as effort and desire. It is a process in which God is with you every step of the way. God's capacity to *give* is as deep as the ocean and as wide as the open sky. Knowing and working with God will take time to change you but make no mistake; *it will change you*. It will change your life *today* and it will change your life *eternally*.

Meditative worship opens the portal to God's loving embrace and influential wisdom. God's Presence, and within it His influence, is, once again, like sunlight. When you pull back the shades and allow this light to permeate your conscious thinking, over time a slow and steady *transformation* takes place within you; a metamorphosis of sorts. When you regularly work with God in this fashion you will acquire a whole host of Godlike qualities and attributes. Gradually and by degrees you will find yourself becoming more and more *like* God. *His* "will" eventually becomes *your will*.

Working with God, like any relationship, is indeed challenging and often times laborious. But when you work directly and intimately with God you will find that the fruits of that labor are *many* and that they are *tremendous*. Here are just a few: God will help you to find yourself, be true to yourself, *believe* in yourself; to celebrate and express your uniqueness and individuality; to discover your talents and help you work to develop them; to do what you *love* and do it *well*; to be imaginative, creative and resourceful; to dream big while at the same time being *realistic* due to a greater understanding of yourself and of the world around you. God will also help you to be optimistic because you know what your life and this world *could be*. He will help you to be bold, confident and self-assured yet soft-spoken and down-to-earth. He will help you to put your priorities in order (first things first). God will help you to develop strong character and positive personality traits such as personal pride, self-respect, self-esteem, self-worth, honor and integrity while at the same helping you to become modest, humble and unpretentious (humility becomes much easier when you realize what perfection looks like). God will help you find the courage to examine yourself (look in the mirror) and give you the strength to *correct* your faults and shortcomings; to look forward while putting the past behind you. God will give you the strength and fortitude for challenges today, within and around you, that in turn give you the wisdom and *maturity* needed the struggles that you will face tomorrow. God will help you to realize that there is great strength in *restraint* and that there is great power in *real love* and in *true wisdom*.

God will help you to understand that while there are some things in this life that are black and white (peace, love, unity, wisdom/ hate, violence, cruelty, abuse) they are many things in life that are gray and brown. He will give you the ability to see the nuance and subtleties in any given person, place, event and situation. He will help you to understand that truth and common sense run side by side as does wisdom and maturity. He will help you to understand that growth and change is measured in *degrees*. God will help you to see more than one point of view; to paint a broader picture beyond the standard frame and expand your thinking; to put yourself in someone else's shoes and walk a mile in them; to not only accept and tolerate differences in others but to appreciate and celebrate them so long as they are positive; to think locally as well as globally; to respect Mother Nature, the environment and conserve its natural resources. God will not only help you with your sense of *self* but also to feel one with the *world* by opening your eyes and ears to the richness and beauty of *diversity* which in turn gives you the opportunity to *practice* love, respect, and tolerance.

God will help you in the exercise of patience knowing that life (progress) is a series of *graduated steps*. He will encourage you to practice true love as well as tough love; to "love your enemies and do good to those who hate you"; to extend the olive branch. He will help you to understand that while it's important to serve others, you cannot lose yourself in the process. He will help you not to throw your "pearls to swine." God will help you to find the strength to say, "No, I can't do that"; to be calm and composed when things become difficult; to anticipate trouble; to be wise about *what* you speak and *who* unto you speak it to (know your audience); to know *when* to speak, when to listen and when to be silent; to anticipate or foresee the consequences of your words and actions as well as your silence; to accept criticism when it is constructive and to defend yourself when it is not; to know what to argue and fight for and what to let go and to be *strong* and *gentle* at the same time.

God will help you to be compassionate without being over-sentimental; to be fair and objective; to put your best foot forward; to do the right thing; to take the high road; to "Do unto others as you would have them do unto you"; to be humble in victory and gracious in defeat; to see the good and positive in everything and everyone; to be less style and more substance; to be real and genuine. God will help you to overcome jealousy and envy and see people more as partners as opposed to rivals and competitors. He will help you to build people *up* as opposed to tearing them *down*. God will help you to become more trusting. God helps you to be your best and helps your best to become *better*. And He will give you the wings to take Goodness, Growth and Giving all the way to Love, Wisdom and Unity.

One of the hardest things to do in life is get a positive ball rolling but once you do, it becomes very difficult to stop. Working with God will help you to get that positive ball rolling by giving you the will-power to break bad habits as well as the motivation to develop good ones. He will help you to be responsible (obligation) and responsible (accountability) for your actions; to be reliable and dependable and have a strong work-ethic; to do a day's work for a day's pay; to be kind and respectful to the people you work for and with; to do your job well and experience the satisfaction of a job well done. He will help you to understand that whatever job you do is important and what you contribute to the whole is valuable.

God will help you to become disciplined and possess self-control. He will help you to take care of the *physical body* that houses your mind, spirit and soul; to become "an ounce of prevention" because it truly "is worth a pound of cure." God will help you to not sweat the little things and make mountains out of molehills; to rid your mind of emotional poisons before they become toxic; to overcome fear while at the same time exercising caution; to know your boundaries and limitations. God will help you to see the value of positive personal relationships and the vital role they play in your development but also to realize that while it's important to have this living support, your growth and progress ultimately depends on *your own sincere effort*. God will help you find the strength and wisdom to makes good choices in life and with them avoid unnecessary heartbreak and tragedy. But when tragedy strikes, God will most certainly help you to *heal*.

Because God dwells within your mind, he works masterfully with your thinking, thought process and *mindset*. This leads to greater over-all mental health, emotionally stability and eventual *self-mastery*. He will help find peace, pursue (and find) true happiness and help you put *balance* and *moderation* in front of everything you do.

There is a calm and peace that comes from knowing God: that there is order and structure to this universe as well as meaning and purpose. God will assure you that no matters what happens in this less-than-perfect world of ours, you are truly safe and secure in His embrace. He will assure you that your life is truly *everlasting* and that beyond this earthy realm lies *eternity*. In knowing God *you will know* that when your life here on earth has ended your resurrected soul will continue living in a new realm and that you *will resume* relations with friends and loved-ones that have gone on before you. And with God you will know that this time apart from them is only *temporary*.

Whether it is a long-term goal or a present situation; from the challenges of raising children and marriage, or the struggles with work or unemployment; to school and studies, friends and family, everything from the smallest things to a death in the family, God is not only there to help you get through them but also to help you *become* stronger and wiser as a result of them. He helps you do everything that you do, *better*. Whether is your relationships or your craft or the organizations that you belong to, you cannot help bringing your spirituality with you to the table.

So you see, knowing and working with God is hardly that "small box" I talked about earlier in this book. It's more like a cargo ship and its contents are constantly delivering peace, love, wisdom and *companionship* straight to your mind and soul in abundance. And this ship is also equipped a compass to help you navigate your way through stormy seas. The journey of life will be difficult at times there's no doubt about it, but in God you will find that there has never been a more sturdy vessel to sail.

The Brotherhood of Man*

. . . and your neighbor as yourself."

The experience of finding, knowing and working with God is indeed a *personal one* first and foremost: you and God alone. But one of the most beautiful outgrowths of that experience/relationship, *when it is real,* is in the way you see, feel and think about your fellow human being. Because of your now intimate understanding of God 's Fatherhood, you gradually but surely come to the rather obvious realization that all the people, no matter who there are or where they reside in this world, are your brothers and your sisters and that the human race is ultimately *one big family.* You begin to realize that it's not "us and them" or "God is on *our* side" but that God is with and within every single one of us and that God is on *everybody's side.*

*I know this statement may be obvious but I am going to state it anyway: "The Brotherhood of Man" does not or should not exclude in any way, shape or form, girls, women or young ladies; people who are gay, bi-sexual, transgendered or any other gender designation. The Brotherhood of Man is *All Inclusive.*

In knowing God, you start to look at people for what is *beneath the surface* of one's skin, clothing and appearance and *beyond the differences* of religion, politics, nationality, culture and language. You begin to understand that it doesn't matter so much whether a person is black or white, male or female, young or old, rich or poor, gay or straight, bi-sexual or transgender. But that which matters most is the content of one's character or in other words, the kind of *soul they possess.* And while God is helping you to appreciate the beauty of *diversity* and the *need* for variety (it takes *all kinds* of different people to move this planet), He is at the same time, helping you to see that *deep down,* we are all very much alike.

We all begin this life as newborn babies. We experience the innocence of childhood as well as the fears and uncertainties that accompany it into adolescence: the awkward changes, growing pains, angst and sexual tension. We all experience the pressures of becoming young adults; of who we are and what we are going to do with our lives into the full-blown responsibilities of adulthood, parenthood and beyond to challenges of our senior years. You see all have weaknesses and shortcomings and that everyone puts on their pants one leg at a time. We share the same anatomy and biological functions as well as being subject to same human emotions: everyone laughs and everyone cries. You realize that we are all subject to sin and temptation, heartbreak and tragedy, sickness and disease, luck (although luck is mostly self-made) and chance, coincidence and circumstance. You understand that no one is exempt from the dangers of life on a material world and the *natural phenomenon's* it produces (the sun shines and the rain falls on all people: "the just and the unjust"). It time you begin to realize that no person is inferior to you or beneath you or your respect. You begin to see that we are all truly *created equal.*

In knowing and working with God, in addition to discovering the many commons traits and experiences that we share as human beings, you begin to feel *true love* and *genuine affection* for every person you meet: a love that is fueled by your relationship and contact (worship) with God. This is the kind love than has that *other person's* well-being and best interests in mind. When you love someone and care about them, chances are you will want to give, share and ultimately *serve* them in a most positive way.

This is the kind of love that changes the *way you live* and that advances your relationship with God. A good way to measure your own spiritual growth is by the amount of love you feel towards other people.

God's love also helps you to see that there is so much more to a person "than meets the eye" and with that there blossoms a desire to really get to know them. It's a love that can appreciate a person's life story: their history and background, their skills and talents, their qualities and potential as well as their pain and sorrow. It's a love that respects their thoughts and ideas, opinions and beliefs. And within this love there too develops and real desire to be caring and compassionate; kind and thoughtful; polite and courteous; warm and friendly; charitable and generous. And by the power of God's influence, what takes place within you is a sincere and heartfelt desire to give to *all people* the love, decency, respect and dignity *they deserve* and that *we all desire*. God's love can and will make this world a more *perfect world*. Once again, perfection is not only our personal destiny: it's our collective destiny.

On a world as diverse, multi-cultural and complex as ours, naturally there will be differences between us. Not everyone is going to be good friends; not everyone is going see eye to eye; not everyone is going to be compatible; not everyone is going to "get along." People are going to rub us the wrong way. But God encourages us to be understanding of our differences and varying points of view and when the inevitable strife and conflicts arise, so too can the spirit of reason and sensibility, sympathy and empathy, tolerance, understanding and forgiveness as well as co-operation and compromise. God also encourages us to discuss the hard issues openly and honestly while the same time being respectful and civil toward each other which can go a very long way towards finding bloodless resolutions to the more serious differences between us. When you love someone, chances are you will be motivated to peacefully resolve the problems between you. This kind of love coupled with unity is what's been missing in this world on a grand scale and is the one truth that will eventually *change this world*.

These truths can go a very long way in mending fences, healing old wounds, bridging wide gaps and removing old walls that we have placed between us to bring about a real, honest, heart-felt and lasting *peace and unity*. When love and unity are fully embraced by the peoples of this world and put in *action*, not only will we understand just what the statement "On Earth as it is in Heaven" truly means, we will see the senseless tragedy and needless suffering on this planet slowly but surely begin to *evaporate* and eventually become *extinct*. It would be a New Age of peace and co-operation that has yet to be seen on our planet. And a love and unity that could pave the way for the return of a great and revered teacher of spiritual truth and true authority on The Father, who walked, taught and healed on this earth some two thousand years ago.

Finding God

"Ask, and it will be given to you; seek, and you will find; knock, and it will be opened to you"

A great many truths have been written about God over the centuries as I have done so here. I could use a million beautiful adjectives to describe the wonders of our Almighty Creator and they would all be true. God is everything I put into these words and so much more. But sixty seconds *with God* will say more than anything or anyone can *about God*. This truth I cannot emphasize enough. As you read these words I say to you, "Do not take my word for it." The greatest love story in the world is nice but it doesn't hold a candle to actually *falling in love with someone*. It's the exact same thing with God. This book can never be anything more to you than a second-hand experience. There's no real substitute when it comes to an active, living relationship with someone. Don't settle! The fact is and will always be that if you really want to *know* what is true, what is good and what is right; if you really want to know who God is and what our Heavenly Father is like, you must open your mind to God's Presence, commit to your soul to Him and *spend the time* it takes to really get to *know Him*. Whoever coined the phrase "Oh My God" was correct. God is *yours*. Take advantage of this perfect being that dwells within you, who loves you and longs to *serve you*. And finally, when it comes to the experience of God, all that He is and all that He has to offer you, this is my one and only request, "Find Him and allow His perfect being to enter yours."

I like to think of God's Presence as a sunlit room with a closed door. The light within this box is God's love, wisdom and influence and the door (subject to your will) is the portal to your mind. When you open this passageway, it allows this light to enter your mind and with that your soul. The wider the door is opened; there more light shines through. This is what is means to not only *experience* God but to *find* God.

To develop and foster a relationship with God or anyone for that matter, you must first find them. This is *central* for true spirituality and something that has perhaps been overlooked over the centuries. God is something or I should say someone that you do not have to travel some immense distance to attain. God has, via His Spirit Presence, done the traveling *for you*. God has the incredible ability to transcend the bounds of time and space to bridge the incredible gulf between perfection and earth to be in *both* places *simultaneously* and He is waiting ever so patiently for the *connection* between you both to be made.

The Holy Ghost is a Perfect Spirit Presence that is not there to criticize, scrutinize, judge or find fault with you; it is not there to threaten, intimidate, manipulate or instill fear in you; it is not there to oppress or enslave you; it is not there to puppeteer you; it is not there to control the environment around you. He is not there to merely *observe* you. God is there to aid, assist and support you; to help you find and *become truth*; to recognize beauty and promote goodness; to expand the positive within you while helping you learn from and overcome that which is negative; to work *through* your mind and *with* you in your experiences to widen your vision, expand your thinking and broaden your horizons; to help you see the common bonds between us; to promote love, respect, tolerance and understanding and ultimately, service. God is there to help you live like God and therefore become Godlike. From your humble beginnings until you reach the glorious shores of perfection, God will be there with you and *for you*.

In God, you will find a *teacher* whose knowledge is whole, whose influence is perfect, whose guidance is true and whose wisdom is complete. In God, you will find a *true friend* and confidant who will always be there for you, who will never let you down and who finds it impossible to betray you. In God, you will find a *parent* who has total trust and confidence in you, who understands you *completely,* and whose devotion, dedication and commitment to you constant and completely *unshakable.* God is a parent whose patience is infinite and whose love for you is unconditional, absolute and eternal. In God you will the Ultimate Being who can love and serve the entire grand universe while at the same time making you feel like an only child. To find God is not to lose yourself: it's to help you become a new and *better you.* To find God is not the end, it's a new beginning. And yes, and I know this is daunting, but *finding* God will not only *change* you, it will change you *for the better.*

If I told you the love of your life lived in the house across the street would you walk that short distance and knock on the door? If I told you that he/she was sitting behind you, would you turn around and shake their hand? Love is a many splendid thing but most of all, love means *being there*. You may have questioned whether or not God is there or whether or not you are worthy of His attention. It has been said that God is so great that He is unfathomable or even unattainable by us sinful, lowly human beings. This is Poppycock! A good parent doesn't say to his/her child, "I am so far above you that you couldn't possibly reach me." A good parent doesn't have a child and then vanish only to return if a list of specific demands and conditions are met. What did your child have to do to garner your love? A good parent never stops loving and serving his/her child even if that child "rejects them." God doesn't wait for us to reach perfection to become involved in our lives. *God is now*! The fact that we are human does not make us unworthy of God's love or render us incapable of finding Him: it is all the more reason to find Him and work *with Him*. The fact that we are human/imperfect makes God that much more *attentive* not only to our present needs but to our future progress as well.

The experience of knowing and working with God is indeed *extraordinary*; finding God however, is not. God is not on a plateau that requires you to solve some complex formula or perform some senseless sacrifice to reach. This is not rocket science. Finding God is one of life's many "rites of passages" that we humans are not only *designed* (tools and abilities) to experience but it's one that we are *supposed to* experience and a relationship that *should be* found and developed. No matter what your background is or where you come from or where you stand presently, you have God and you are equipped to find Him. And always, always remember that God *is on your side.*

He is not only on the side of the poor and sick, weak and pitiful, oppressed and downtrodden, he is on the side of the rich and famous, handsome and pretty, powerful and privileged. God is on the side of presidents and prime ministers, chancellors and emperors as well as vagabonds and hoboes, paupers and peasants. He is with the Communist, the Marxist, the Socialist and the Capitalist. God is with the educated and uneducated. God is with the blue collar, the white collar and the black and white collar. He is with the religious and non-religious. God is with the Jew and the Gentile. He is with the prostitute, the pimp and the John. God is with the addict just as much as He is with

the dealer. He is with the gang member and the
policeman. God is with the judge, the prosecutor
and the defendant; He is with the victim as well
as the perpetrator. The Father is with the violent
as well as the peaceful; He is with the humble
as well as the arrogant; He is with the loving as
well as the hating and He is with the honest just
as much as He is with the corrupt. No person is
above or beneath our Father. In God's eyes, no
one is too high and no one is too low. Regardless
of status and social standing, God is with (within)
you. Our Heavenly Father, once again, is *incapable
of anything less.*

I once saw a bumper sticker that read, "God
is my co-pilot." And the more I thought about it,
the more I realized that this statement is spot-
on accurate. But even that is contingent upon
you opening the *cabin door.* There is a doorway, a
gateway, a portal that exists between your conscious
mind and God's Presence. If there wasn't this
barrier, everyone would know God instinctively,
which certainly isn't the case. Just ask anyone who
doesn't know or want to know God. God will not
break down this door in the same way you cannot
force a person to open up (break down) and *allow*

someone to give them the love and support they desire to give to them. It is *their choice*. God, being the lover of freedom and freewill, has put that door there for a reason: it is there so that we may open it willingly of our own *accord*, by our own *effort* and of our own *freewill*. No one can do the actual work for you, but someone or something can certainly help you accomplish this.

To comprehend the nature and essence of God is perhaps simple. But to dig down deep within and peel back the layers of pain and hurt, sadness and desperation, doubt and skepticism is when things can become a bit more challenging. We can easily get down on ourselves and think of ourselves as unworthy. How could anyone stand by me and stick with me with all the things I've done? We are prone to harbor feelings of anger, guilt, doubt, worry, fear and frustration. As people and over time we can become stubborn, selfish, arrogant, lazy and complacent. There are also the issues of environment and upbringing. There is no question that there are many factors that can work against us in our quest to find what it is that we seek and be who wish to become. But the same obstacles that hinder our ambitions can also be used as *motivation for change*. Whatever the case may be, always, always remember: regardless of what might be in *front* of your doorway, *nothing will change* the Presence of God that dwells *behind* it. You don't change God; God changes you.

Nothing God is and nothing God gives is forced upon you. A person can make a thousand mistakes in a row without God interfering. God is so gentle, so subtle and so unobtrusive that He is seemingly non-existent until you make that *connection*. A neon sign doesn't look like much of anything *until you plug it in*. Then it becomes brilliant, bright, bold and vibrant. This is what takes place the *moment* you plug into God and is something that I am personally reminded of every single time I become *one with God*.

If "The Kingdom of Heaven is Within You" ultimately, you have to *go within* to find it. Finding and experiencing (becoming one with) God requires a few things. It starts with *will* and *desire* and is achieved through hard work, effort and due-diligence as well as intense *focus* and serious *concentration*. Opening the door requires a combination of heart *and* mind, emotion *and* intellect working together in *concert*.

When I found God, I was a carefree (perhaps too carefree) happy go-lucky eighteen year-old kid without a worry in the world. My mind was a "clean slate" religiously speaking so my discovery of God was rather easy and happened very quickly. This certainly is not the case with everybody and may not be the case with you. Maybe right now is not the best time for you because you've got a lot on your mind or life a bit stressful and that's O.K. This may not happen immediately. Do not be discouraged. God will wait *as long as it takes* for you to make this connection. If you keep on digging, eventually *you will hit water.*

Your Discovery

"Whatever becomes your catalyst, your relationship with God will be incomplete until you open yourself to God's Presence within and allow His Perfect Spirit to enter your *conscious mind*."

What good are the most eloquent speakers with all their theological knowledge or the tall buildings with their amazing architecture and colorful glass windows if at the end of the service you feel no closer to God? What good is the fancy nightclub with its fine crystal, plush carpeting and exotic drinks if at the end of the evening you leave feeling the same way you did when you arrived there: alone. Social interaction is nice but it's poor substitute for a one-on-one, personal, intimate living relationship with someone (God). The *core truth* of this *entire book* lies within these next few paragraphs: where belief becomes reality, where theory becomes fact and where a living relationship is born and from that day forward you will *never feel alone again.*

So far in this book you have read words on paper and hopefully they have moved you in a positive way. God is right now; right this second, hard at work within you. He is not only *tirelessly working* to influence your mind and with that your soul; He is *waiting* ever so patiently at your door for you to welcome His loving Presence into your *conscious mind.* Because words will always fall short, to *know* God, to truly *know* His importance, value and magnitude, to *experience* His love, peace, wisdom and beauty *first-hand*, this channel between your mind and His spirit *must be opened*. This event changes *everything* and is the single most important reason why I am writing this book. Hopes, dreams and aspirations are vital and important but that is all they will ever be if *action* isn't taken. Now the time has come for you to take action and to begin working on finding and experiencing this amazing, perfect Presence for *yourself*. Start with something simple. Go for a walk in the park; observe a sunset; stare into the stars on a clear night and see first-hand the magnitude of God's infinite creation; spend some quality time with a good friend; maybe you could give of yourself and *help somebody*. These activities may not open this channel completely but they can give you a glimpse into the depth and beauty of the Almighty and align your thinking with that of God's to make this door within you a bit more *transparent*.

As I stated earlier in this book, there are many sources and techniques that help a person to truly connect with God and tap into the Mind of God. My suggestion for you is this: When you feel that you are truly *ready* and that the time is right *for you*, set aside just a little bit of your time. Find a place, home or away, that is quiet and with limited distractions; a place where you feel safe, relaxed and at ease. Once you've gotten yourself comfortable there and have cleared your mind (probably the most difficult exercise in connecting with God) of all the everyday thought clutter, start to shift your thinking towards the spiritual. Maybe start with positive things; about the people and places and experiences in life that have moved you in a positive way: events or people that have given you a taste of God's love and essence. And when you feel ready to, steer your thoughts to directly *to God*: things you know either instinctively about Him or truths that someone has told you about or the truths that you have perhaps read in a book. Have a conversation with God. Talk plainly and candidly to Him about His Spirit Presence that is right there waiting ever so patiently to be discovered and experience *by you*. And ask God directly, "Are you here?" "Are you within me?" and "Do you love me?"

Connecting with God on this level is a *discipline*. The more you *exercise* these mind muscles and the stronger they become, the easier it becomes to open this channel. And the more you open this door, the more you will come to know and understand God and the more He will be able to positively influence you and ultimately transform your entire being.

Afterglow

What you will experience *first* in finding God is real and unabashed *love*: love that is gentle and tender as well as powerful. It is an *embrace* that will surround you with its warmth and resonate throughout your entire soul. When you discover God, when it's *real*, His love for you is so intense and so moving that there is *no mistaking* the experience for anything else; it is simply that *powerful*. It's a lot like the day you met that person who you discovered is a lot like you and will probably become one of your best friends; or when you met that special someone, fell in love with them and experienced their love *for you in return*; or when the doctor handed you your newborn baby for the very first time; or getting that pat on the back and the reassurance that everything would be alright. These are the people and events that you never forget. They are etched in your mind permanently and will burn in your heart forever. When you find God, don't be surprise to wake up the next day not only a changed person but with the whole world looking a whole lot different.

"With God, all things are possible"

I have a dream. My dream is for you to tell me about God. Not because of what you've read or what someone has told you, but because it has come from something you have lived and experienced. My dream is for you to *know these truths*, to feel them down to your bones and right to the core of your soul. My dream is also to witness the true "coming of an age" in this world. My dream is for people from North America to Europe, from South America to Africa, from Asia to Australia to find God and change this world of ours; I dream of a world where politicians are unified to serve *every person* in their nation; I dream of a world that is without hate, without violence, without prejudice, without discrimination and without iniquity; I dream of a world where war is a thing of the *past* and that *wherever* there is hate and conflict it will be resolved through *love* and *wisdom*. My dream is that one day we all come to the realization that we are *one people*, under God and *unified* by His love. And these dreams *will come true* when this world is awakened to the love and wisdom that flows ever so freely from *our* Almighty Heavenly Father to all the people of this earth. Amen.

CPSIA information can be obtained at www.ICGtesting.com
Printed in the USA
BVOW02s1517030215

PP6125500001B/1/P

9 781425 957599